FACING FEAR

STEP OUT IN FAITH AND RISE ABOVE
WHAT'S HOLDING YOU BACK

NIK WALLENDA WITH
DON YAEGER

W PUBLISHING GROUP

AN IMPRINT OF THOMAS NELSON

Facing Fear

© 2020 Nik Wallenda

Published in Nashville, Tennessee, by W Publishing, an imprint of Thomas Nelson.

Thomas Nelson titles may be purchased in bulk for educational, business, fundraising, or sales promotional use. For information, please email SpecialMarkets@ThomasNelson.com.

Any internet addresses, phone numbers, or company or product information printed in this book are offered as a resource and are not intended in any way to be or to imply an endorsement by Thomas Nelson, nor does Thomas Nelson vouch for the existence, content, or services of these sites, phone numbers, companies, or products beyond the life of this book.

Unless otherwise noted, Scripture quotations are taken from The Holy Bible, New International Version®, NIV®. Copyright © 1973, 1978, 1984, 2011 by Biblica, Inc.® Used by permission of Zondervan. All rights reserved worldwide. www.Zondervan.com. The "NIV" and "New International Version" are trademarks registered in the United States Patent and Trademark Office by Biblica, Inc.®

Scripture quotations marked KJV are taken from the King James Version. Public domain.

Scripture quotations marked NKJV are taken from the New King James Version®. Copyright © 1982 by Thomas Nelson. Used by permission. All rights reserved.

ISBN 978-0-7852-3429-6 (audiobook)
ISBN 978-0-7852-3428-9 (eBook)
ISBN 978-0-7852-3427-2 (TP)

Library of Congress Cataloging-in-Publication Data

Library of Congress Control Number: 2020939955

Printed in the United States of America

20 21 22 23 24 LSC 10 9 8 7 6 5 4 3 2 1

To my wife, Erendira, for your selfless love
and support, as we've literally walked
the highs and lows of life together.

To my kids, Yanni, Amadaos, and
Evita, whom I pray for daily as you
courageously pursue your dreams.

To my sister, Lijana, who inspired me to truly
understand what it means to never give up.

—NW

To Will and Maddie. I hope you have the
friendship and partnership that Nik and
Lijana developed. Face fears together!

—DY

CONTENTS

FOREWORD

THE OPPORTUNITY TO SPEAK IN SARASOTA TO THE members of Bayside Community Church in August 2019 was one I was excited to accept, but as usual the opportunity turned out to give me more than I was able to give the congregants.

At the end of the first service, I was heading back to the greenroom they had set up for me when the lead pastor asked if he could introduce me to one of his church members. It was Nik Wallenda. I have to admit, I knew some of the legend of his amazing family but didn't know as much as I should have of Nik's personal story. Yet as he began telling me about his life, his sister, the accident, and how they had walked Times Square . . . I found myself leaning in. I was locked in and couldn't wait to hear more.

He shared how the journey had taught him more about facing fear than any previous experience in his life. This from a guy who walked over Niagara Falls and the Grand Canyon!

I was in full learning mode.

I kept thinking the same words but didn't want to

interrupt. Finally he hit a break in the story and I just blurted, "Have you ever thought about writing a book?" I could only imagine that if he could rivet me in that thirty minutes, I would absolutely sit down and read any and every word he had to write.

"I've written one," Nik said, "but I'm getting ready to write another. I just can't find the right cowriter."

I knew whom he had to use and connected him immediately to Don Yaeger.

But just as quickly, I told him he needed to get going on his third book. I wanted to learn more about his amazing marriage and all that it takes to build a relationship like the one he shares with his wife, Erendira. The support they offer each other and the way they follow their faith into challenging times make theirs a marriage I wanted to learn more from.

"Let me get through book two first!" Nik said.

I was a fan of the Wallenda legend before the greenroom. I'm a greater fan today and can't wait to continue growing while helping Nik share his story.

This is a book we all can use. I am honored to have a small piece in helping it come together.

—John C. Maxwell
May 2020

CHAPTER 1

THE FALL

ONE BAD EXPERIENCE. THAT'S ALL IT TAKES.

A bad week. A bad day. A bad moment. One wrong step, and suddenly the world is upside down, spinning out of control, and before you know it, nothing is the same.

That's what happened to me. I was in a circus tent in Sarasota, Florida, the place I call home between my different adventures. I'm an aerialist—a wire walker—and I make my living by placing one foot in front of the other and trusting my training and my skill to keep me alive. But one day, things changed when I put my foot on a wire as a part of a world-record-attempt eight-person pyramid . . . and we fell.

Suddenly, nothing was the same.

Maybe you've had a terrible experience that caused you to fall, to question all that seemed stable in your life. Maybe you grew up with an abusive parent or are in a relationship with a manipulative partner. Maybe you had a fight with a loved one. Or accepted a new job only to find out your boss is harsh and overly demanding. Maybe you were in a car accident or experienced a sudden illness or financial downfall you never saw coming. Maybe it was a virus that rocked an entire world.

Whatever your circumstance, this book is for you. It's a book about fear—something we all face. Fear that tells us we're not good enough to do whatever we were made to do. I'm writing it for you because I want to share what I've learned from a long and hard-fought journey.

THE WALLENDA LEGACY

In 1978, my great-grandfather Karl Wallenda fell to his death from a high wire strung between two buildings in San Juan, Puerto Rico. He was in his seventies, old for a wire walker, and the rigging of his wire just wasn't right.

In the video footage, you can see him sit down and then start to grab the wire—something that we have been trained to do for generations. The wire is our safe spot. But once he got down to the wire, he didn't have the strength to hold on. Doctors told our family that there was such a surge of adrenaline to his heart, it overwhelmed him and quite possibly caused him to go into cardiac arrest—in turn, he fell from the wire. We are sure his age and several previous injuries were major contributors to his not being able to handle the adrenaline rush.

Doing the one thing he was trained to do to keep safe led to my great-grandfather's death.

I grew up watching that video because my parents

were wire walkers too. In fact, they met because my great-grandfather recruited them both to be part of his troupe. Back then, there were still plenty of circuses that traveled the world, and the Great Wallendas were a big draw for many. My family's patented style of aerial courage—working without the safety of a net—was always a highlight of any show.

We were superb at it. So much so that when I was barely two years old, I climbed onto a wire for the first time. My mother remembers watching me atop the practice wire in our old backyard, how I patiently climbed up to the wire (which was only two feet off the ground) and then quickly stepped out onto it.

It didn't take me long to fall. But I picked myself up, got back on the wire, and tried it again. That's also what we do. Mom said it took me no time to get the hang of it. It was as if I were born to walk the wire.

In the years since, I've come to that exact conclusion—I was born to walk the wire. As a believer in God, there's no such thing as chance to me, so my family's background, history, and culture were all necessary ingredients that I would need in order to become who God designed me to be.

I grew up hearing the stories of our family's calling, the dangers of risking our lives to show people what is possible. I heard about the small accidents that caused injury and about the big accidents that killed members of my family. We told those stories as a way of remembering the past, but even more so as a way of staying focused in the present, because when you perform on a wire, there is no room for fear. That's what my family believed, and it's what I grew up believing too.

One of the stories that we frequently told happened in Detroit in 1962. My great-grandfather was a pioneer in the aerial arts. He was constantly inventing new and amazing feats that could be done on a wire, and one of his most outrageous stunts involved seven people in three tiers—four walking the wire, with two people balancing atop them, and another person balancing atop those two—as they moved across the wire. He called it the seven-person pyramid.

The act became an immediate sensation, and Great-Grandfather brought his troupe to Detroit to perform it at the Shrine Circus in the Michigan State Fairgrounds Coliseum. In front of a crowd of seven thousand people, the Flying Wallendas took to the wire strung thirty-five feet above the coliseum floor. While there's no video of the incident, there are accounts that someone cried out, "I can't hold on anymore!" before the entire group toppled and fell to the ground.[1]

Two of the troupe members, Richard Faughnan and Dieter Schepp, were killed. Richard was my great-grandfather's son-in-law, and Dieter was my great-grandfather's nephew. Jana Schepp, Dieter's sister, fell onto a circus ring mat, and so her injuries were not overwhelming. My great-grandfather's adopted son, Mario, was paralyzed from the waist down, and my great-grandfather injured his pelvis and sustained other injuries (though he snuck out of the hospital the next day to perform his contracted show at the same circus).

I grew up hearing that story, looking at the photos captured that night, listening to how my great-grandfather learned to cope with the emotional and physical trauma by bravely moving on, keeping his word, and fulfilling his contract. I learned from my family that falling—and the danger of falling—is a part of life that I couldn't focus on because it would create fear in my mind, and if that fear took hold, I wouldn't be able to walk on the wire.

My family wanted me to understand that danger *is* part of our history, but because we're carrying on a legacy, shutting out fear is what we do.

Usually when I share this with people, I get some strange looks. People don't understand how you can just shut out fear, but I promise you, it becomes very normal.

You see, after years of training, I don't see what others see: that every time I get on the wire, I risk my life. It is to me what elements of everyday life likely are for you. Chances are you don't think that every time you get into a car to drive somewhere, you're risking your life. You don't see that every time you cross the street, you are putting your life in the balance. But the reality is that there are risks in *everything* we do.

The truth is, I could die from choking on something just as surely as I could die from falling off a wire. That's the risk that comes with life, and no matter what we do or don't do for a living, we all make our peace with it in some way. I don't think a small business owner or accountant gives his family a hug and a kiss and says, "See you tomorrow," or "See you tonight," while simultaneously thinking, *I may never see you again.* I don't think firefighters or Uber drivers head out on a call thinking, *This could be my last run.*

We compartmentalize some of the dangers we face because compartmentalizing is helpful to us. According to the Wharton School, it's a major component in our ability to take any kind of risk: "Compartmentalizing enables a person to identify what is stressing them out and to allow other, unrelated factors in their life to stand on their own merits."[2] All of us have the ability to push things to the side in order to focus on other things that matter to us—the things we call everyday life—and the only difference is the type of everyday life we grow up living.

For me, everyday life was walking on a wire. It was setting aside the fear of falling. It was going out and putting on the best show possible. From the time I was little, I knew I wanted to be an aerialist like the generations before me, and I threw myself (literally) into their training. I was taught how to find my center of gravity, to feel the wire with my feet, to breathe, and to master other essential skills that make it possible to walk on a tightly suspended wire dozens of feet above the ground. And being in the family business has been my life for forty years now.

The older I got, the better I became. I eventually started performing on my own, with a troupe of friends and family that I recruited, and we cut our own path. While my parents struggled to keep the business alive due to the decline in circus attendance, I opted to take the family business to the masses in a new way: television. Although people were not attending the circus in person as much as in the past, they were more than willing to let the circus come to them through the magic of television. That simple shift is how I successfully built my career while holding fast to my family's traditions—all with the intention of creating enough excitement to attract a new demographic to the circus and under the big top.

It's also what led to Sarasota and the fall.

REBUILDING A PYRAMID

One of the themes of my career has been replicating some of the more famous acts from my family's history. I mentioned earlier how my great-grandfather Karl Wallenda died from a fall in San Juan, Puerto Rico, in 1978; well, my mother and I successfully completed that exact same walk together in 2011 as a way of honoring him. In July 1970, he walked across Tallulah Gorge in Tallulah Falls, Georgia, and I performed a similar (albeit larger) stunt when I successfully walked across Niagara Falls in June 2012.

There have been echoes of my great-grandfather's career all throughout mine, including the infamous fall that changed the lives of our family: the Detroit pyramid. We re-created that walk in Detroit in 1998 with a team that included my uncle Tino; my mother, Delilah; my father, Terry; and some other relatives.

In 2017, my troupe and I were preparing for one of our next big events, a world-record attempt for my hometown crowd: an *eight*-person pyramid walk performed at a greater height than ever before. After successfully duplicating the seven-person pyramid, we'd expanded the act by one, which sounds trivial but dramatically changes the dynamic of how the formation balances and moves. The stunt was going to be challenging even with the best wire talent I could recruit. We set up in my backyard (as we have always practiced in our backyards for generations) and began rehearsing months ahead of the performance.

We were located in Sarasota, which is home to a lot of circus performers and has readily accessible rehearsal space. We advanced to practicing in the Circus Sarasota tent because we had trained down low and it was time to rehearse up high in the actual setting prior to having an audience. The tent was large, with a blue interior, the stands encircling the outer perimeter.

We'd been in the space for a while because the process of the eight-person pyramid requires some specific training progressions: you slowly raise the height as your group gets accustomed to each level. We'd pushed ourselves all the way to twenty-eight feet above the ground and were feeling good about our work thus far. In fact, I was feeling as good as I'd ever felt.

My faith in God and my team seemed unshakable to me, and I was enjoying the blessing of God like I'd never felt it before. My relationship with Christ means everything to me—*is* everything to me. I lean on him for guidance in all things, at all times, and I live my life to bring him glory. He made me to walk on a wire, so I am obsessed with being the best aerialist in the world. I take seriously 1 Corinthians 10:31: "So whether you eat or drink or whatever you do, do it all for the glory of God." With my stunts at Niagara Falls and the Grand Canyon, and with numerous other world records bringing so much media attention to my work, I felt like the eight-person pyramid was going to be my next great accomplishment.

I felt all of that deep in my soul as I looked each of my teammates in the eye and asked them if they were ready for another walk. Each person—from Aunt Rietta to Andrew to Alec to Zeb to Nicholas Slimick to my cousin Blake to my sister, Lijana—looked back at me with confidence and declared they were ready. We were developing a deeper level of trust than I'd ever known in a troupe, and even though three of them were literal family, I saw each member as more than a loved one, but as someone I trusted my life with, someone I cherished and praised God for. I was excited for what we were doing, how we were pushing boundaries with excellence and skill while continuing to honor my family legacy of going bigger, higher, and further.

———◆———

I wish I could tell you exactly what happened next. I wish I could rattle off, with absolute clarity, the fateful moment when things changed for my team and me. Even as I write this, I'm still processing it, still trying to pull the images, sounds, and emotions together to form a sensible story. Although I can relive and replay it at any time from memory, I wasn't in a spot to clearly see what the cause of the accident was.

Instead, what I have is the sound of multiple balancing poles colliding. I hear them smack together with too much force, and I feel—without necessarily seeing it—the entire team stop moving at a moment when movement is essential. I feel a slight tremor in the wire, and then I see nothing else but chaos.

Everyone falling.

Arms and legs flaying the air.

The blue of the tent top.

The sound of bodies crashing against the cold, hard floor.

As I'm brought back to the moment, I feel the cold wire biting into my arm. I'm grabbing the wire for life but looking down at a reality I still find hard to process.

Andrew, who had been standing on my shoulders, lies motionless on the ground twenty-eight feet below me. My sister, Lijana—one of the best aerialists I know—lies on the ground as well. Likewise for Aunt Rietta. The same for my friends Alec and Zeb.

I am hanging, helpless, above them as they are scattered on the ground below. Thinking about it now, this is where my fear took root—in that suspended moment of help-lessness, as I was hanging between what I thought I could control and the madness of what was below me. I wasn't in control of anything, wasn't sure of my place, wasn't sure what to do or how to respond. That, to me, was the seed of fear, and it was planted right then into my heart without my knowing, without my realizing. There's a verse from the book of Job that captures that exact moment in a way I couldn't at the time:

> What I feared has come upon me;
>> what I dreaded has happened to me.
> I have no peace, no quietness;
>> I have no rest, but only turmoil. (3:25–26)

My great gift is in ruins beneath me. The sight pulls me into the moment, and somehow—though I don't remember how—I pull myself up onto the wire, make my way back to the platform, and then climb down, forcing my body to bend to my will so I can check on everyone. When I finally get to the ground, Andrew is closest and I go to him. "I've broken a lot of bones," he says, "but I'm okay. Go to the others."

My eyes then lock onto Lijana's face. When I get to her side, my heart sinks; Lijana's face is mutilated, her arm mangled. I cradle her in my arms, my insides bursting with a mixture of pain and uncertainty. I lean my head down to hers, and she whispers to me to go check on others.

Gently, I let go of Lijana and run to Zeb. He is in and out of consciousness. "Stay with us, Zeb," I plead. I kneel by his side until his eyes open, and then I race over to my aunt. Rietta is in excruciating pain but doesn't appear to be in danger of losing her life.

But Lijana does appear so—and in fact is.

Looking at her, I fear losing her, so I make my way back to her and keep asking her questions: "What year is it? What is your son's name? What state are we in?" I manage to keep her talking, but as she speaks, teeth and blood spout from her mouth. Her face contorts as it swells, and her voice wavers as her lips quiver uncontrollably. In the distance, sirens scream as ambulances and emergency personnel arrive. Within minutes, the paramedics are working the scene, moving from person to person, tending to the chaos.

Family and friends begin to arrive. Soon, news helicopters are overhead, but I don't worry about them. Instead, I walk outside to an ambulance and climb in beside Lijana. The doors close with a thud, and we drive off, the circus tent getting smaller in the distance.

The ride to the hospital is just a blip in my memory now, but the chaos when we arrived is clear in my mind. Doctors and nurses surround my sister and pull her from the ambulance, and I see that Andrew and Zeb are being ushered inside as well. I look for a place to land, uncertain of where I need to be, uncertain of what I will learn from the doctors in the hours to come.

I learn that Alec and Rietta were loaded into other ambulances and were taken to different hospitals so as not to overwhelm the trauma center.

As people race around, I withdraw from it all, tucking myself off to the side with little to offer in the way of help. I lean my head against a post and close my eyes, only to have flashes of the fall jump into my mind. I think about my great-grandfather, about the night when he watched as his seven-person pyramid fell, and I wonder if he felt just as helpless.

I sink into a chair and do the only thing I can: wait. My phone has been ringing off the hook, but suddenly I see a call from Alec's cell phone, and I immediately answer. He tells me that other than some bruising on his feet, he's fine. That's one, but what about the other four who hit the ground? The moments drag by until finally the head of the Sarasota Memorial Hospital Trauma Center, Dr. Alan Brockhurst, approaches; he looks around, makes eye contact with me, and immediately updates me, explaining that Andrew required surgery but is out of danger of losing his life. Zeb was bruised up, and they're sending him for a CT scan to be sure he doesn't have any internal bleeding, but he appears to be okay. Dr. Brockhurst has also called the neighboring trauma center for an update on Aunt Rietta; she has broken a hip, leg, and arm, among other injuries, but is in stable condition.

But when I ask about Lijana, he says he will have to get back to me with her status.

After a miserable fifteen minutes, Dr. Brockhurst finally comes back with the news: Every bone in her face is broken. Her kidneys and liver are bleeding. He explains in a serious voice that her injuries are significant—they're going to put her into a medically induced coma—and he will keep me updated but has to get back to attend to the injured. I still have so many questions for the doctor swirling through my mind: *Will she survive? Will she have brain damage? Will she ever be the same again? How many surgeries will it take?* The list goes on . . .

Soon enough, others arrive—friends and pastors and family. Everyone has questions. My friends are there to support me in any way. The pastors are there to lift my family up in prayer. The family members just want to be there for our injured loved ones. I take each group in turn. I hug friends, I pray with the pastors, and finally I take my place with the family, sitting and staring at one another, none of us knowing what will happen next. Overwhelmed with emotions, at some point I fall asleep in the waiting-room chair.

A BIG DECISION

When I woke up in the waiting room the following morning, my father came over and sat down beside me, his eyes focused somewhere in the distance. I wondered if he was mad at me; I'd asked Lijana to join me in the pyramid, and now she was in the hospital, seriously injured, and we were not even sure if she would survive. I wondered if my father might take that anger out on me—not because it's his nature, but because he's a father, and fathers protect their children, even from their other children. Instead, my father took a deep breath and said, "You have a decision to make."

I looked at him. He still looked straight ahead.

"What do you mean?" I asked.

"Tomorrow night. At the Amalie in Tampa. You have a performance."

Amalie Arena is where the Tampa Bay Lightning play professional hockey. I was scheduled to do a speech while walking a high wire for It Works!, a multilevel marketing company owned by a friend of mine. As I stared at the emergency room filled with pastors, family, and friends, getting back up on a wire was the furthest thing from my mind.

"I don't know," I whispered.

My dad nodded and patted me on the leg. He stood and walked to another set of chairs, sitting down beside some other people. I turned to my wife, Erendira. Like me, she's a performer, and a brilliant one at that. We've been privileged and blessed to do some amazing things in our lifetimes, so if anyone could understand what I felt in that moment, she could. She looked at me, her eyes open, her heart ready. I looked down the hallway toward Lijana's room, and I took my wife's hand.

"I don't know" is all I said. I kept everything else I wanted to say or that I was thinking bottled up.

The hours ticked by slowly, and a lot of people came to me to talk. I said a lot of things to many people, most of which I can't remember, but what stuck with me was the feelings I had inside me. Feelings with which I was entirely unfamiliar. Because of how I grew up, I didn't really know how to define them—they weren't fear as much as disgust and despair. Disgust that I'd somehow lost control of the moment; despair that I'd somehow devastated the people closest to me while escaping injury myself. I was a wreck, and in the back of my mind was my dad's voice, reminding me that there was a show tomorrow night—and in our family, in our culture, the show must go on.

Up until that moment, I'd never canceled a show. As a Christian, I am a man of my word, which means if I sign a contract, it's a promise I will keep. I'm passionate about it because it's a matter of integrity to me; I want to be a man who honors his commitments. But that night, I seriously considered canceling. My mind was so messed up that I wasn't sure I'd be capable of walking on a wire ever again, more out of respect for those who were injured than out of fear. One of the keys to successfully walking is to keep your thoughts under control; you have to block out the negativity and the what-ifs and focus on the things you know are true. You have to keep your mind disciplined at all times.

But there in the ER, I was failing that test. I kept asking myself—asking God, really—why God would allow me to survive with little more than a scratch but would let Lijana and the others get broken so badly. The guilt of my survival washed over me like a wave, and I couldn't find the surface, couldn't breathe under the weight of the emotion. No matter where I turned, there was no escaping the horror of that fall. The world I knew, the world where I felt in control, was gone. In its place was a world where so many people were in pain. I didn't know how to orient myself accordingly.

Later that evening, I pushed to see Andrew. Once I was in his room, I looked at my friend and said, "If you don't want me to perform tomorrow night, I won't. Just say the word, and I'll cancel it without hesitating."

Andrew looked at me for a moment, his face unreadable. I wasn't sure what I expected him to say, but I wanted to give him the chance to say something, anything, even if he tore into me over the accident. I'm not sure if I was looking to just get the conversation of my blame over with, but I was prepared to accept whatever came out of his mouth— except for what he actually said.

"That makes zero sense. I think you're crazy, but of course you should walk the wire. Go do what you always do and make us proud."

I'd love to tell you that Andrew's answer set me free, but it didn't. If anything, it plunged me even further into the unknown. His words felt right, but I was still willing to cancel; I was lost, adrift in this new world and desperately looking for an anchor I couldn't find. And that sense of being adrift only amplified the disgust and despair. Suddenly, a way of life I'd managed to avoid crashed into my world and wrecked so much of what I believed.

I had always believed that many people were gripped by fear because they *focused* on fear; they focused on their issues or on their negative thinking, and it blotted out everything else. As a Christian, I knew that God went before me in all things, so I was always able to go confidently out of the house. In fact, that's one of the challenges I always had when I spoke, especially to the nonreligious world: How could I convey that message without being too overbearing as far as my faith? It's just who I was: "Let all your thoughts be known to God" (Phil. 4:6, my paraphrase). So that's what I practiced.

But now, that practice, at least in the moment, seemed worthless.

I thanked Andrew and left his room. I got home late into the night and fell asleep, exhausted. When I woke up, my pastors and managers and I decided to do a press conference rather than have reporters dog everyone connected to our family or the victims. And it was obvious I was the one who needed to step up and face the questions.

I talked with my dad, then went to the circus tent for a midmorning press conference. I still didn't know why we fell, and I didn't want to answer the questions of a bunch of strangers when I had too many questions of my own. As a Wallenda, however, I stood there and took each question and answered as best I could.

No, we don't know who or what caused the fall, and I won't assign blame anyway. Yes, I'm aware of my family's history and the fall in Detroit in 1962, but no, I don't see any connection, and I certainly don't feel as though my family is cursed. "If anything," I said to the reporters, "my family is blessed." Blessed that we have the fortitude to regroup and move forward, blessed to be part of a family and a tradition where tenacity prevails.

The final question was the one I answered most confidently: Yes, the Wallendas would be represented at the Circus Sarasota later that night. Because the show must go on.

YOUR PATH THROUGH FEAR

Not long after the last question was asked and answered, I made the drive to Tampa. I got up on the wire at Amalie Arena with a microphone strapped to my shirt, and I walked above thousands of people. I can't even tell you everything I said; I just know that it poured out of me, a cascading testimony about God's goodness even as I felt my insides churn with anxiety. As I walked, I cried, and when I sat down on the wire at one point, I could see hundreds of people in the crowd crying with me. It was a spiritual experience to talk about my faith in God while walking on a wire and dealing with the aftermath of what had happened just two days before. In my heart and soul, I knew I wasn't all right, but being back on the wire gave me a sense of normalcy—a sense that everything would be okay. I know that denial is one of the five stages of grief, but I'm not sure that's what I was doing right there; I think it was more about me finding that anchor I would need to survive the chaos.

It makes sense that the place where I felt the most stable was on a wire. After all, it's what I'd known my entire life.

I had told reporters at the press conference that the show must go on, but I would soon find out that stability and healing aren't the same. When we suffer a tragedy, after the initial shock our next instinct is to find any path forward. But what if there is no path in sight? I've come to learn that the show doesn't go on for some people. For them, the show stops the day fear invades. There's no pressing forward in faith. There's no summoning of courage. There's just the persistent, powerful fear that locks out the world.

Whatever your situation, you're the reason I wrote this book. I've experienced both ends of the spectrum: I've walked the pathway of faith and have been stopped in my tracks by paralyzing fear. But there is a way forward through fear, a pathway that God lays out before us. It's a pathway we see time and time again in the Bible, in the stories of Abram, Moses, Joshua, Joseph, David, and Jesus. It's a narrow pathway to be sure—maybe even as slim as the width of a nickel, just like my wire—but it's one you can walk too.

And who better to help you learn to walk it than a seventh-generation Great Wallenda?

CHAPTER 2

THE SECOND FALL

IF WE'RE GOING TO GO ON A JOURNEY FROM FEAR to faith, it makes sense to understand what I mean when I talk about fear. At the time of the accident in Sarasota, I didn't fully understand what I'm about to share; it took me a long time after our pyramid collapsed before I could grasp it. You may disagree with me, but I can only share with you what I learned from my experience and some research.

There are two types of fear: healthy and unhealthy. As human beings we're wired for both, so let's take a moment to talk about them and how they impact the way we live.

First, there's healthy fear. This is the *experience* of fear— it's that instinct implanted within human beings to help us navigate a dangerous world. We all experience fear in some way, shape, or form whenever we encounter circumstances that prompt a stress response in our bodies.[1] It's a physiological response that's commonly called the fight-or-flight response.[2] That experience keeps us from drifting too frequently into danger and protects us from the genuine perils of the world.

Then we have unhealthy fear. This is the *emotion* of fear—the psychological response to uncertainty or danger—which is where so much of our dysfunction begins. It's when our minds play tricks on us and warp the world in ways that make it unrecognizable. The emotion of fear doesn't protect; it prevents. It prevents us from moving forward. It prevents us from healing. It prevents us from being who (or all) we were created to be.

Growing up, I was familiar with the first kind of fear. Being raised in a family of aerial performers, I had full awareness of the healthy fear. It was something I encountered whenever I set foot on a wire—not just because I could feel it, but because my family would reinforce it with me. Fearlessness isn't helpful on the wire; but courage is, and my family deeply believed that courage was the outflow of being prepared. So we trained and drilled and practiced like no one else in the business, learning to account for almost every variable there could be once we were on the wire.

I carried that belief with me into adulthood; even on the night we fell, I wasn't scared when I set foot on the wire because we were working on our craft. We were doing what we needed to do to be safe on the wire.

Whenever I talk about this with other people, they inevitably look at me funny. There's such a fine line between the two kinds of fear that most people never recognize it, so it's hard for them to really get what I'm trying to say. Fortunately, there's a great book that can help make the distinction clearer: the Bible. If you dive into Scripture, you can find both types of fear—the healthy, respectful, protective fear, and the kind that renders people helpless.

Proverbs 1:7 says, "The fear of the LORD is the beginning of knowledge, but fools despise wisdom and instruction." This is the first kind of fear—the kind that helps keep us safe. We know that because the writer of the proverb, King Solomon, connected healthy fear with knowledge. He was saying that respectful fear is wise and opens us up to wise choices; to drive that point home, he offered a contrast in the second part of the saying: "fools despise wisdom and instruction."

There are plenty of other verses that reference this kind of fear, often positioning it as deep respect or awareness. In Genesis 22:12, when God stopped his servant Abraham from sacrificing Abraham's only heir, Isaac, God said to him, "Now I know that you fear God, because you have not withheld from me your son, your only son." In Exodus 1:17 we read about Hebrew midwives who refused to follow Pharaoh's command to murder baby boys because they "feared God."

The second kind of fear is easier to spot. You see it in Joshua 5:1—after God performed a miracle on behalf of his people, the enemies of Israel "melted in fear and they no longer had the courage to face the Israelites." The angel Gabriel spoke of this version of fear when he appeared to Mary, the mother of Jesus, and startled her. "Do not be afraid," Gabriel said, "you have found favor with God" (Luke 1:30). Jesus even used it in John chapter 6, when he walked on the water toward his frightened disciples (who thought he was a ghost) and called out to them, "It is I; don't be afraid" (v. 20).

In Exodus 20:20, we get a really good example of both

kinds of fear. Moses, who was leading the enslaved Jewish people out of Egypt, told the gathered crowd, "Do not be afraid [unhealthy fear]. God has come to test you, so that the fear of God [healthy fear] will be with you to keep you from sinning."

Now, those are a lot of Bible verses, but they help make my point: there's the kind of fear that helps us know the truth about our circumstances, and then there's the kind of fear that is a liar. And not just any liar, but an obnoxious liar. It lies well. It lies loudly. It lies persuasively. It lies often. Pretty soon, that fear is the only voice we can hear, and it blinds us to the truth.

That's the type of fear my family wanted to protect me from, because it can take your life on the wire. That kind of fear distracts you from focusing on the details and technique required to keep you safe; and if you're not solo on the wire, that kind of fear can harm your partners as well.

So I grew up without that kind of fear. We simply didn't allow it. The healthy fear we embraced and discussed because it made us smarter and sharper while we performed. My parents taught me to call it out, face it down, and practice until I mastered my physiological response to it. I'll get deeper into this later in the book, but it took years to develop that kind of mastery, of being able to take my physical sense of fear and put it into a compartment separate from my conscious mind. While other people my age were wrestling with unhealthy fear, I was sailing safely past it, learning instead to hone my craft, perfect my footwork, refine my balance, and take control of the fight-or-flight response so it became nothing more than an idea, easily countered and easily dismissed.

I'd love to tell you it's a flawless system. But it isn't. And sometimes it's costly.

NO TIME FOR QUESTIONS

After the opening of the Circus Sarasota, I routinely visited the hospital to check on Lijana. She spent her fortieth birthday in a medically induced coma in the ICU, and we were still uncertain what her future held. As her brother, I was not only worried, but I was also struggling to process everything. There were naturally questions about the incident, and they ranged from the practical to the spiritual.

The practical questions were hard to answer because of the fog of trauma. The spiritual questions were hard to answer because I'd never had to ask them before.

As a believer in God, I trust him completely. I believe he has full sovereignty over everything in the universe. That word *sovereignty* trips a lot of people. They think that means God causes everything to happen, which naturally means they want to know if God caused the accident. They want to know why he would do such a thing.

Sitting in the hospital, I was asking similar questions. It didn't take me long, through prayer and pastoral counsel, to come to my conclusion: God didn't cause the accident. Arriving at that absolute conviction served me well during those early days in the aftermath. There was a massive challenge on my horizon: a seven-person pyramid act, this time at the Big Apple Circus in New York City. Only a week before the accident in Sarasota, we'd signed a contract to appear in the Big Apple Circus starting in December for a six-month run, which meant I had to get myself back into the right mental space to get back on the wire. But while that was a "future" I had to prepare for, I also had a very important decision about the present: Circus Sarasota was a four-week-long contract, and the accident happened two days prior to the opening of that run. We decided to move ahead with the Sarasota engagement but deliver only an abbreviated performance using the artists who were not physically injured during the fall. Then we had three months off before heading to Atlantic City to perform and train for shows there and in the Big Apple.

Knowing what was ahead, I reminded myself that we live in a broken, imperfect world, and sometimes things just go bad. Sometimes things happen that are horrible, tragic, and painful, but they're no more caused by God than they're caused by bad luck or a black cat crossing your path.

I took those questions, along with the answers I felt I understood from my prayers, and I put them into a compartment, just like I'd always done, just like I was taught. I couldn't carry doubt with me because doubt opens the door to unhealthy fear, and I had performances coming up; I couldn't afford to be emotional with everything that lay ahead of me. While some people might suggest I was in denial, I think of it as going numb; I turned off the psychological pathways that would allow fear to overwhelm me, and I chose to just forget about it. I couldn't see the benefit of trying to assign blame—either to someone on my team or to God.

After the Sarasota run was complete, I went to work assembling a new team for New York. I'm sure no one would've blamed me had I tried to cancel that contract or reschedule the event, but I was determined to make it work. One of my greatest strengths is my integrity; if I make a promise, I keep it. Others may be flexible with their word, but I believe that I honor God when I keep my commitments, and New York wasn't going to become an exception, no matter how exceptional the circumstances.

Besides, my family's credo was *The show must go on.* And so it would.

With my family members sidelined for the foreseeable future, I began searching for other aerialists with the kind of skill necessary for the seven-person pyramid, which was a difficult task. Wire walkers are never readily available, which is why we look for people with the skills we need and rigorously train them (a great lesson from my mother!). And now we were on a schedule that was tighter than I preferred. The pyramid is a challenging, intricate act that needs months if not years of preparation to ensure that the team knows one another, knows the routine, and knows the wire and the feel of seven people moving as one.

I'll be honest: when it comes to who I'll step onto a wire with, I am unapologetically demanding. I want people whose professionalism and skill are equal to mine because that's the level of performance required to do what I do. But as I searched for my New York team, I realized I had to be a bit more relaxed in my demands or else I wouldn't have a team. As a result, I took on some walkers who weren't as seasoned as I wanted. All of them were good people—I

27

wouldn't have hired them otherwise—but compared to my family and my usual caliber of partners, they were definitely a group that would need some high-pressure seasoning.

Unfortunately, seasoning takes time, which was something we didn't have. But I was determined to make it work, so I pressed on. I signed a contract to perform at the Tropicana Casino in Atlantic City, New Jersey, where I also made arrangements for the troupe to train every day leading up to the performances—in an air-conditioned setting! The casino also would cover housing and food, so financially this was a huge benefit. We booked out a few months of rehearsal and set a start date.

I was still doing smaller contracts that kept me in Florida so I could drop by the hospitals to check on Lijana and Rietta. Zeb and Alec were released within a day after the accident. While the others were making progress, Lijana struggled. There were times when I would sit outside the hospital and burst into tears, then quickly dry my face so I could go in and see her.

Writing this now, I can tell you I was a mess, but at that time, I didn't know what I didn't know. I only knew what I'd always known, which was to push forward, keep working, and make sure the next show not only went on but went on flawlessly and without incident.

Before long, I was in Atlantic City, and we were up and running. The initial phase of training for the seven-person pyramid is a dry run on the ground, where everyone learns their positions. It's a time for people to get to know their teammates in front, behind, above, and below. Once that's established, it's on to an on-ground run where people climb into actual position, learning how to pass one another the shoulder bars that we use to create the levels of the pyramid. After that, you head to the wire, starting only two feet above the ground and moving up as you get accustomed to the sensation.

I'm compressing a lot of information here, but this was an extremely stressful time for me. I was away from home, breaking in a new team, and Lijana still wasn't out of the woods.

SHOW BUSINESS

Worrying about my former teammates who were recovering from injuries while training new ones wasn't the only pressure I was facing. Additional stress came from making sure the show was perfect. I always have to satisfy my own demanding nature when it comes to any production that bears my name. To put it bluntly, I was thinking about business and making sure it didn't go south.

I'm a little bit different from other performers because I understood early on that the circus was a dying industry. Just take a look at Ringling Brothers, the best-known circus in the world, a circus that first brought my family to the United States in 1928. Ringling Brothers shut its doors for good in 2017 after years of declining revenues and seemingly endless court battles.[3] When a circus struggles, it's always the performers who take the hit; it's not uncommon for some circus acts to make as little as $2,500 a week, which sounds like a lot until you realize they're doing ten to twelve shows a week, risking their lives for what's essentially $250 per show, and then having to split that between multiple performers and use it to cover travel, medical, food, and other costs. It's about the same pay that my great-grandfather was making roughly forty years ago, because that's the way circus life is—it's barely changed because a lot of those performers were born into it. It's what they know, and they have a lot of pride in doing it well. But, sadly, they don't get the chance to do as well financially as people in some other professions.

That is a part of why I have tried to take circus life to a new plateau, if you will. I want people to see those of us who love the performance art of circus differently. That old definition of circus life is, if I can be so bold, one that I knew I didn't want, going all the way back to my teenage years. As a kid, I remember watching my parents struggle, not because they weren't smart or savvy, but simply because the circus life was their passion. I remember looking at other professional athletes and thinking, *Why can they make so much money? What makes their athletic achievements more valuable than ours?* I'd look at Michael Jordan or another superstar on TV advertising for Nike, and I'd dream about the day when Nike would design a shoe for me. But beyond that, I began to make mental notes that would shape my future. I realized that while the skill sets were different, my family and I were just as much athletes as the guys on TV. So why shouldn't we get paid like them? After all, we are risking our lives on top of being athletes. And if you can do something better than anyone else in the world, if you can do something that's nearly impossible for every other person on the planet, you should be paid more.

So I decided to change the narrative for myself. I began

marketing myself and my skill set as an extreme athlete, and later as a performance athlete. I made other people see me differently, and it opened doors for some great partnerships with ABC, NBC, the Discovery Channel, and other networks. It allowed me to step into the world of reality TV and learn about broadcasting and producing a television show. I've been blessed to do prime-time specials and serialized shows, and one of the biggest sources of pride for me is that if you see my name attached to the project, you can rest assured that it's going to be done with excellence. When you see my name as an executive producer at the end of a show's credits, that's effectively my personal signature guaranteeing that it was the best I could possibly make it.

It has come at a cost, mind you—there are some folks within my community who don't care for the route I've chosen. They don't like the cameras, the production, or the fact that I wear jeans out on a wire. To them, it's a betrayal; to me, it's an evolution that has allowed me to keep my family's legacy alive and well. If I have to give up circus costumes in order to help the masses learn to appreciate the skill and artistry of what we do, then so be it. (I like wearing jeans anyway.)

I share all of that to say that the pressure I felt leading up to the seven-person pyramid walk in Atlantic City was exponentially greater than anything I'd faced before.

NEAR THE END OF MY ROPE

I can be persnickety even when things are good—like I said, I do everything with excellence, whether it's cleaning my kitchen or putting together a performance—but with the time crunch, the new team, the trauma of the accident, and my habit of compartmentalizing everything, I became a different person, and it showed. The training in Atlantic City was abysmal; I was short with people, pushing them hard, demanding they learn things the way I wanted them to. It got complicated, especially when I found out that someone was out late drinking the night before practice, or I had to break up arguments between team members. I was pushing myself harder than I'd ever pushed before, and it naturally spilled over onto them because I wanted them to feel what I knew deep down in my bones: that their behavior didn't just impact them; it impacted all of us. Their sloppiness or inattentiveness or interpersonal tension contributed to a lack of focus, and a lack of focus created danger. My safety—their safety—rode on being attentive, committed, and diligent. That's the way my family had always taught me, and that's the only way I knew to do things.

But I wasn't dealing with my family.

Nothing drove that point home more for me than when one of my team members quit after the show closed in Atlantic City and we were two weeks out from dress rehearsals in New York City. We had transitioned our training to a tent at the fairgrounds in Sussex, New Jersey, and after months of training, he suddenly started shaking on the wire, which caused me to immediately stop practice and pull him aside. He looked me in the eyes, said, "Sorry, Nik—I can't do it," and walked off the stage. I didn't bother to go get him; there was no way I could build his confidence enough in a few short weeks.

I emailed everyone I knew, reaching out to anyone who'd ever worked in the industry, looking for a fill-in. I ended up bringing in someone who had been working in Japan. Amazingly enough, he'd done the seven-person pyramid before, but only in practice. And he hadn't done it in years. I flew him over and put him in the lineup, and within a few minutes I realized something was very wrong. He walked a little differently than my family did; he was a Spanish-style wire walker, which meant that he found his center of gravity and balance in a way that was completely different from the rest of the team. While the rest of the team was holding their backs completely stiff in order to create a good base for the people above us, he was moving his hips all around to try to keep his balance. That one difference created a pyramid that moved; even with everyone else holding as still as possible, his small hip gyrations made everything sway. So I had to break his lifetime of wire-walking habits and train him to walk like the rest of our team.

And I had to do it in two weeks.

I dove in, looking for his strengths, looking for what he did well that was similar to what we needed him to do. To borrow a phrase, I went looking for the gold and ignored the dirt; once I had something good I could identify, I began encouraging those good habits. I've found that encouragement produces a better return than criticism, so I leaned into that leadership strategy. When he got frustrated, I would say, "You're doing great. You're solid, you're strong, you're consistent, but I need you to tighten up your hips. I need you to make this minor adjustment so your strengths can emerge." In a short amount of time, he got smoother, the pyramid got steadier, and we were able to move efficiently and effectively as a unit.

I would love to tell you that after that I could breathe, things got better, and the show went off without a hitch. But that didn't happen. Four days into his training with us, the new guy came to me and said his grandmother had died, and he needed to leave to be with his family. I'd just spent $8,000 to bring him over from Japan and rush his work visa, and he was asking me to advance him the money to fly out for his grandmother's funeral. He'd be gone for four days and come back with only four days left before our first show.

I kept my composure long enough to agree to send him to his family and fly him back, but that didn't last long. The very next day, what was left of the team was rehearsing, and things just didn't feel right. And before I knew it, I lost it. I blew up at my team, stormed out of the tent, and stomped to my truck. I got in, slammed the door, and started driving into the middle of the New Jersey countryside. To this day, I have no idea where I was going or what I hoped to accomplish. I can only tell you I wanted to get away.

I parked the truck in a little field and leaned my head against the window. Suddenly, everything bubbled up. The fall. The pressure. The fear. I stared out the window and realized that while I'd stuck my unhealthy fear in a box, it didn't mean that fear wasn't affecting me. I called my friend and manager, Winston, who is also a close confidant and a fatherlike figure to me. I blurted out all my frustrations, and the truth came to the surface, into the full light of day. Winston, who had witnessed my blowup with the team, listened patiently and then shared what changes he'd seen in me, changes that concerned him.

"Nik," he said. "You haven't dealt with the accident in Sarasota."

I didn't say anything.

"Nik? Did you hear me?"

Sitting in my truck, I put my hand to my head.

"I don't know what's wrong with me, Winston. I don't know what's going on."

As the sun hung low over New Jersey, I realized that my training—my lifetime of putting my fear into a box and pretending it didn't exist—was failing me. I was going to have to do something drastic, something I didn't know how to do, and I was going to have to do it fast.

I had to confront my fear and learn to deal with it.

Or I might never walk a wire again.

CHAPTER 3

KNOWING IS
NOT ENOUGH

AFTER I TALKED WITH WINSTON, I MADE THE LONG drive back to the fairgrounds. I called Erendira, and she advised me to call the other members of the troupe and ask them to meet with me when I returned. I made those calls as I drove, and by the time I got back, the entire team was waiting for me. There were some skeptical looks on their faces, along with a lot of hurt. Truthfully, we hadn't been getting along well as a team, and my outburst only made that fact all the more obvious. We went out to the middle of the fairgrounds and sat down in a field to talk.

I looked each person in the eyes and drew up the courage to say, "Guys, I'm sorry. I don't know what's going on. I don't know what's gotten into me."

There were a few nods of understanding, so I continued.

"I'm going through something mentally, and I have no right to treat you the way that I did."

I looked at Dieter when I spoke, since he had been the one who took the brunt of my frustrated outburst. Dieter was staring at me, not unkindly but almost invitingly. And it was then that I broke down.

The stress and trauma of life since the accident came spilling out of me in a way that was different for me. I'm a very transparent person; I've nothing to hide, and I wear my heart on my sleeve. But I'm also a very reserved person. I'm not prone to dumping my emotional baggage on other people because I'm usually the person who helps others carry the load. It can cause problems at times, but it's a side of my personality that developed as I acquired the discipline necessary to perform on the wire.

As I've mentioned, I was good at compartmentalizing my feelings because there's no room on the wire for baggage—you have to be clearheaded and focused. Even if I got into an argument with my wife right before a performance, we would leave that argument on the ground, *never* bring it onto the wire. But I was struggling with compartmentalizing as a response to the accident, and that came to the surface in the middle of that fairground. I told everyone how sorry I was, how I needed their support and help, and how together we would get through this.

It was a remarkable moment. I'm the kind of person who immediately forgives when someone does something to me. I don't hold on to grudges or any kind of negativity because that becomes one more emotion that has to be compartmentalized. There's only so much of that I can take, so I choose to forgive quickly and keep things rolling. Because of that, I get embarrassed when I'm the one who needs to be forgiven. It's a shame thing—a mixture of guilt for my actions and confusion over what drove me to behave that way. Sitting there with my team, I was feeling all of this—embarrassment, shame, guilt, confusion, fear—and I couldn't see a way forward. Even as I told them we could get through it together—which I genuinely believed—I had no idea how that would even be possible.

Emotionally undone before my team, I felt the weight of Winston's words to me. I hadn't dealt with the accident at all. I'd been numb for months, and now, for better or worse, everything I'd been burying was out and alive and in front of me.

The question was, what would I do with it?

FACING MY WORST NIGHTMARE

I want to take you back for a moment to the days after the accident, because that's where the problems really began. I want to dissect those days so you can understand how easy it was for me to simply bury everything—but I also want you to see how so many people choose to do the same. As human beings we have a limit on our abilities to respond to traumatic events. At some point, if we don't stop to deal with what we're experiencing, we slip into the numbness that derails us down the road. It's what psychologists call *depersonalization-derealization disorder*, and while it's often brought about by substance abuse, it's also a common response to severe or intense distress.[1]

I can't say that I was experiencing depersonalization-derealization disorder, but I can say that I was under a serious amount of stress, not only from the accident itself but also from the way I had to respond to it. With my team scattered around different hospitals, there was a feeling of constant chaos—no one was where they should be, and I was limited in my ability to be everywhere at once. Further complicating matters was the attention being paid to Lijana's condition and the status of the other injured members of the troupe. And when I say attention, I mean it—helicopters hovering over the hospitals, news crews parked outside the emergency room doors, trauma surgeons walking out to address the cameras and give updates on everyone's conditions.

I remember being at the hospital when Winston called me.

"Everybody wants to talk to you," he said.

"I know."

"You should probably talk to them."

"I know."

There was a pause.

"You know, you could just lie low and let me deal with it."

I took a deep breath. Letting my manager face the fires has never been my style, but it was tempting at that moment. Lying low was attractive to me, but it's not how I work. In my career, I've always faced the music, good or bad, and running away after the worst possible thing happened felt like the wrong move.

"No," I said. "That's not how I do things. I think I should talk to the media."

"Okay," Winston said. "We'll figure it out."

Kerry Sanders, a journalist from NBC, ended up flying into Sarasota. I first met him in 2008 during an appearance on *Today*, and we became friends off-air. Winston had Kerry's crew come to the lobby of Lijana's hospital, and we set up the interview there. He was the only person I spoke to the day of the accident, and the interview ended up going on *NBC Nightly News* and then aired again the next morning on *Today*. Once I talked with Kerry, everyone else wanted to hear from me as well. The requests poured in, and my publicist began to campaign for a press conference.

Mind you, my sister was still in unknown territory; the doctors weren't sure at all how she would respond. Meanwhile, I was being squeezed to come out and talk to the world about our fall and what it meant. I'd barely had time to process what had happened, much less anything else, but the pressure was on.

It got so intense that I called my pastors in Sarasota, Randy Bezet and Burnard Scott, and asked them to meet me at my RV, which served as my on-site greenroom and dressing room. Because it was right behind the tent where the accident happened, it was easy for us to slip away to meet together and pray. Early in the morning, they arrived and we prayed for Lijana, Andrew, Alec, Zeb, and Rietta, and we asked God to give me the wisdom to stand up and speak out. There was a quiet knock on the door from my publicist, and I knew it was time.

Forty-eight hours after we fell from the wire, I walked with my publicist back into the tent where the accident happened. There was still a mess on the floor—stains from where people had bled and where others had tried to clean up. A crowd of reporters were gathered with thirty or forty cameras and lights and microphones, and I had to walk right over those stains to get to them. It was a surreal moment. It was honestly the hardest thing in the world for me to do because I had to pass over the spots where people dear to me had lain injured and talk to reporters as if everything was okay. And as I was walking, I relived the accident—the slap of the balancing poles, a sudden gasp of air, the wire bouncing furiously, and me, hanging there, looking down at my sister and my family, helpless to reverse any of it.

By the time I reached the reporters, I had fully compartmentalized my feelings. I spoke with the press for almost an hour, answering question after question about what happened, who was hurt and how badly, what I was feeling, and what was next for my family. When it was over, I didn't go back to my RV or find my wife for a moment alone—I went right back to the hospital, found a chair, and poured myself into it. My dad took a seat next to me, and we sat there in silence, him thinking about who knows what, and me thinking about never getting on a wire again.

I share all of that with you because I want you to know what happened: I didn't have space to process any of it. I didn't have time to accept that the accident was real. I was moving so fast and doing so much that there was a dreamlike quality to the whole thing. Sure, I was sitting in a hospital waiting room as my sister fought for her life, but I was fine—she was the one fighting, not me. The accident happened to her, Rietta, and everyone else, not me. I was a survivor. I got away unscathed.

At least, that's what I thought. The truth was that I

didn't get away unscathed; I just didn't have an injury anyone could see. And because of that, I was expected to continue on like I always had. I was expected to walk the emotional tightrope of trauma by simply putting one foot in front of the other and choking back my fear and doubt. But often, physical injuries heal much more quickly than mental ones.

THE SHOW ABOVE ALL ELSE

I often think back to when my great-grandfather fell in 1962 and how many of his family were killed or injured. He suffered a double hernia from the fall and was dealing with catastrophic loss but still snuck out of the hospital to go perform the next day—which is insane to some people but just the way things are when you're a Wallenda. This is what makes us some of the best aerialists ever to perform; we are dependable and consistent.

If I'm being honest, it's not just a Wallenda thing; it's a circus thing. If you were to ask anyone who is a circus performer or grew up in that culture, they'd tell you that they are the hardest working, most reliable people you could ever meet. They don't call in sick. They don't show up late. They don't phone it in—because it's been ingrained in them for generations that the show matters more. It is both a blessing and a curse.

I've worked on days when I didn't feel great. I've worked on days when I wanted to stay in bed—days when I was running a fever or had a cold so bad I could barely breathe. I've held the seven-person pyramid with a fractured ankle for weeks before seeing a doctor, fully aware that he wouldn't have let me perform if I had seen him right away. I did this in order to fulfill a contract; the show must go on, and there's no backup I can call. There is no safety net for me—not only literally but figuratively. If I don't hit the wire, if I don't make the show, then there's no one behind me who can pick up the slack. And if I don't perform, I don't get paid, and my family doesn't get to eat. While I've gone to great lengths to ensure that my circumstances aren't the same as my ancestors', I'm still a performer, which means I have to perform if I want to earn a living. This is why I'm so fastidious about my health. Everybody else in my life can get sick and take a day off, but when I'm being paid to give a speech from a high wire above 3,500 people, I can't call the temp agency and ask them to send a replacement. These are the terms of my life.

I can articulate these things now, but I couldn't then. Instead, I kept doing what I had always done: stick to the training that made my family and me successful. I can see now that it wasn't helpful to me—it was putting a Band-Aid on a gaping wound. All I knew to do was keep moving, keep moving, keep moving, but all the while I was reliving the accident. It would go through my mind at random times, and I would recall various images. I would always try to block out the accident, not allow myself to dwell on it, because I knew it was a weed.

Negative thoughts are like weeds growing in your garden; if you don't pull out the weed, it will just lead to more weeds popping up until they overwhelm what you've planted. It's the same with negative thoughts. But in trying to fight off those thoughts, I kept pushing the accident and its effect on me further and further into my emotional basement until, finally, I exploded on my team in Sussex at the fairgrounds and found myself in the New Jersey pastureland wondering what was wrong.

It's the double-edged sword of strong conviction—your strength can become a weakness when overused. The line between being reliable and myopic is thin; the distinction between being attentive to details and obsessive-compulsive is subtle. Before the accident, I wasn't even aware there was a tipping point, but sitting there in the middle of the fairgrounds, confessing out loud that I was not doing as well as I thought, the reality of where I was emotionally hit me. I was broken, and I would need fixing, and it was not going to be as simple as it used to be. I could no longer ignore the truth about my life—that danger was present in every step—but I also knew I couldn't give in to those fears.

That's essentially where I left it with my team that evening. I admitted my brokenness, my uncertainty, and my need for healing. In being vulnerable with them, I opened the door for us to clear the air about other issues. We talked out the problems we'd been ignoring, and then we literally hugged and made up. The bond we'd been missing over the weeks of rehearsal was suddenly reborn in the middle of that field.

I'd love to tell you that I was reborn that evening, but that was far from the case. At our next rehearsal, I noticed the wire was shaking. We were in formation for the pyramid, everyone was in their places, and the wire was trembling under my feet. There's always some small amount of movement in the line—that's just physics—but this was far more pronounced, the kind of shaking that only happens when someone isn't solid in their technique. Some of my teammates called it out immediately, but I didn't say anything. I cataloged it for later because there was no way we would be able to perform the act with a teammate shaking the wire like that. I would sooner cancel the contract for the show than go out with someone who was putting the entire team at risk—and I don't cancel contracts. Honestly, the shaking unnerved me, but I was determined to keep going.

But it happened again the next day. And then the next day. And the day after that. No matter how many times people called it out, the wire kept shaking, and it started to affect everything. Someone on the team was unsteady, and after a week or so of letting it slide, I made up my mind to address it. I was going to have to root out the person who was putting us all at risk. The next time we went up on the wire, I decided to stop everything the moment the wire vibrated in the slightest and identify the culprit who was putting us in danger.

We climbed to the platform and arranged ourselves in formation. I watched everyone like a hawk, keeping my eyes on their form, their footing, the way they moved the equipment. They looked steady enough, but I knew someone was working hard to hide the shakes. We got everyone up and into place when I felt the shaking again. I knew I had to say something, to confront the person creating the tremor, but I stopped short.

I realized the person shaking was me.

All of my training, all of my experience, all of my history

were worthless in that moment. I was afraid—and I felt it all the way through my body. There was no compartment where I could stuff it anymore—it had taken root in my mental garden and was revealing itself in full force, choking out every other thought.

What I knew to do with that fear was no longer enough. I had to find a way to face it and defeat it without making it my focus.

Of course, I had no idea exactly how to do that.

CHAPTER 4

SILENCING SHAME

ONE OF THE BIGGEST LIES WE TELL OURSELVES IN moments of crisis is a very simple sentence that's easy to believe: "No one will understand."

It doesn't matter if you're surrounded by people who know and care about you, or how deeply connected you are to your family, friends, and coworkers; that one little lie can creep into your mind and disconnect you from everyone who loves you just when you need them most. For some people, this sense of disconnect can become a full-blown mental illness; for others, it's just a sense of estrangement they carry with them because they know something that no one else does.

It's a difficult place to be, if for no other reason than it can sometimes feel like there's no way out.

Once I realized I was trembling on the wire, things began to change for me. The corner I thought I'd already turned ended up curving longer and wider than I could've ever imagined, and the sense of shame and loneliness that came over me was intense. I didn't have the option of literally hiding myself away, so I opted for spiritually hiding. Though I continued to pray and seek God the way I always had, I became distant from the people around me.

Fortunately, they did not become distant from me.

That's the benefit of being part of a community—of having family and friends who know you. In my case, not only do they know me, but they intimately know the life of a performer as well. One of those people—in fact, the best of those people—is my wife, Erendira. She not only understood what I was going through but also knew the lens through which I was seeing it, and she knew my mind and heart. If there was anyone on the planet to whom I could turn for insight, it was her. And it still took me days to do so.

When I finally decided to talk to Erendira about what was going on, I discovered she had already noticed.

Before I could open my mouth, she confronted me, saying, "You're shaking."

"Yes," I said, acknowledging the obvious and the uncomfortable.

"What's going on with you? What's wrong with you?"

"I don't know. I don't know what's going on. But I'm certainly not comfortable." I paused. "And I don't know that I can do this anymore." There was an awkward silence. I had never said the word *anymore*.

Some people will tell you that admitting your doubts is helpful, but I wasn't in that camp. I felt so defeated mentally. It was something I'd never experienced before, which only amplified the fear. I wish I could paint a compelling picture of how it felt—the sense of being overwhelmed that came with every unwelcome thought. It was like being trapped in a swarm of insects, and fighting each thought was exhausting. Nothing that I'd tried before was working; I was no longer able to just shut out the fear, and the nerves and uncertainty were now translating to the wire. In every way possible, I felt weak.

Erendira listened patiently. Growing up as a performer and in a circus family, she had a sense of what was going on. Both of her parents come from circus families—her mother's in Australia, her father's in Mexico. Erendira grew up learning stunts and feats, which is part of why we work well together—she knows the danger in what we do and isn't put off by it. She doesn't love the wire the way I do, so she performs other stunts that are just as dangerous. But she'll tell you the teaching is the same: you stare down the fear; you don't give in to it.

When you watch her, it's easy to believe she's fearless—something I know firsthand from her record-breaking 2017 iron-jaw hang 300 feet above Niagara Falls. She literally suspended herself by her teeth from the bottom metal hoop attached to the bottom of a helicopter that hovered over the falls. The record she broke was a 250-foot hang . . . performed by me.

As far as I knew, Erendira had never felt fear in her life. But when I started talking about what I was going through, she told me about a panic attack she had during one of our stunts. We were opening the season at Foxwoods with a wire act, and she began having difficulty breathing. For an asthmatic, being short of breath isn't anything new—but what was happening that night felt different. Standing on the platform as the act began, she just blanked; she described it as feeling like blacking out, where she couldn't hear the music or pay attention to what was going on around her. I was on the wire with her and had no idea; she was literally sitting on a bar that I was supporting with one other performer, and I couldn't tell she was in distress.

She never talked about that night with me because she felt like it was hers to handle alone. We're both believers, so we know that pride is a sin, but when you're struggling on the wire, it's not pride that keeps you quiet. It's almost a protective instinct—the belief that if you talk about it to other performers, you'll somehow infect them with your thoughts. It's what I was dealing with in New Jersey—but it's also why I eventually went to her, and it's why she was able to understand.

"I just want you to be safe," she said. "If you feel like you can't do this, if that's what you truly feel, I support you."

And then she let me know how much she understood, how much she truly supported me.

She said, "Let's cancel the contract."

There was so much happening at once, so much I couldn't control, so much I couldn't make right, that the appeal of killing the deal was definitely there. If I canceled the contract, I wouldn't have to worry about training people or what they did on the wire. Most of all, I wouldn't have to worry about my shaking. But the appeal of covering up my struggles were outweighed by what I would lose by canceling: my income, my reputation, my sense of self. Giving in to my fear wouldn't just cost me the wire; it would cost me something much, much greater: my integrity. It was a price I couldn't pay.

I looked at Erendira and said, "No. Let me try to work through it more. Let me give it a few more days."

She nodded. "You don't think canceling is the right idea?"

"No. I think I can get through this. I don't feel as though I'm going to fall; I'm just trembling, and it's not good."

After talking with Erendira, I felt a little bit better, but it didn't last. A couple of days went by and rehearsals were okay, but I still wasn't completely myself. Part of the reason was trauma, I'm sure, but the other part was the conditions for the New York routine. In my entire life, every time I've done the seven- or eight-person pyramid, I've never had a safety net. We just don't use that stuff. My family has always taught that safety nets provide a false sense of security; my great-grandfather had a brother fall into a net, and he was still killed. While the rigging and technology have changed a lot over the years, the truth is that no matter what you do for safety's sake, nothing is 100 percent guaranteed to work. Even the best gear doesn't always keep you safe. My whole life that truth has been drilled into my mind, so much so that I've accepted it. Safety is on me, not the net.

By law, New York requires a safety system in place for any high-risk performances, and the circus we signed with wanted us to use an airbag as well. I had never trained or performed with an airbag before, but no matter how much I would've preferred to change that, it was one of the rules. Everyone wanted us to have some kind of safety mechanism, and it was with that safety mechanism that I experienced true fear on the wire.

Please understand: I'm not against safety. I prepare and train with safety in mind at all times—I'm constantly thinking about where I am, what I'm doing, and how it impacts the wire and the other performers. Those are all elements that I can and should work diligently to control because they have the most bearing on whether I stay safe. So when I say I felt true fear on the wire for the first time in New York, it had nothing to do with the quality of the safety; it had everything to do with how that safety rigging impacted me mentally, which was that it did nothing for me. It didn't make me feel safe or protected—quite the opposite. Most people would think, *Well, he's got a safety net, so now he can relax! Everything's good.* But that just wasn't the case. The extra equipment, the extra responsibility, and the change in routine only made things worse for me, and I struggled as a result. The net made me so much more aware of the risks, so I was focusing on the risks and not my skills and training. My shaking got worse, which compounded the shame I felt, which further spiraled my fear. I felt completely out of control, out of sorts, and out of options.

A couple of days of repeatedly bad practices tipped the rest of the team off that something wasn't right. Dieter, the teammate I had confronted in that argument, pulled me aside after practice and said, "Nik, what is going on with you?"

I avoided the question, asking, "What do you mean?"

"There's something wrong," he said. "I don't know what's going on with you, but you need to snap out of it."

He grabbed my shoulder and shook me as he spoke, almost as if he were trying to literally snap me out of the funk.

I just went back to my RV and sat there thinking. I remember asking myself out loud, "What is going on with me?"

It was another example of how alone I felt. Few things shake you to the core like someone else pointing out what you thought you were hiding. I knew that if Dieter was asking me what was wrong, the rest of the team was aware of it too. It undid me—I was supposed to be the leader, the one everyone else looked up to as an example. And yet I wasn't projecting that sense of leadership; I wasn't inspiring confidence in my team because I was struggling with confidence in myself. Not in my abilities, mind you—walking the wire is second nature to me, as much a part of me as my blood—but more in my confidence to overcome the unknown. If I was unsure on the wire, how could any of my team feel safe? It was a textbook leadership challenge.

I don't remember his exact words, but what Dieter was saying to me was this: "You're not who you've always been. We've always looked up to you. You've always been so inspirational, you've been the leader, and you're not that person on or off the wire. There's something wrong with you!"

Even his simple observation that something was wrong reverberated in my head and amplified my shame. I sat in my RV thinking not that something was wrong with me but that *I* was wrong.

That *I* was broken.

That *I* wasn't capable of being fixed.

It was another confirmation that I had more going on than I even realized. I was trying to hold it together on the outside and act like everything was great, but the reality was that inside I was a mess. I wondered how I had gotten to that point. And I came to the realization that I was allowing thoughts of falling and thoughts of the accident to flood my mind whenever I was in the tent. I was worried about what happened to Lijana happening to someone else, or something like what happened to my great-grandfather happening to a member of my team.

Then I realized I was also worried about what happened to *me* happening again.

Growing up, I believed two things: God was in control of everything, and I was in control of what I did. I was taught the faith part by my parents, and I was taught the second part by my community. My faith in God had always been unwavering—I've trusted him since I gave my life to Christ when I was three years old—and my trust in my abilities was something I'd never doubted. The fall in Sarasota was a storm, a trial that shook my faith as well as my confidence and forced me to reexamine both, to really look deeply at what I believed. It was a call to stop and assess my internal and external worlds in order to make sure they not only aligned but were founded in something solid. I was experiencing a spiritual battle as much as a mental one.

Suddenly, it all made sense. I believe that humanity has an enemy who is out to destroy every person on earth. His name is Satan, and he wants to separate us from God and from the life God designed each of us to live. The Bible calls Satan "a roaring lion looking for someone to devour" (1 Peter 5:8). He's crafty (Gen. 3:1) and deceptive (Rev. 12:9), a murderer and a liar (John 8:44). While he's often popularized as a character in a red suit with a pitchfork and horns, the truth is much more terrifying: he's a manipulator who can challenge our very understanding of the world and our place in it. One of his biggest weapons, one of his best strategies, is to separate us through a cloud of shame, to lead us into thinking that no one could understand us, and that the reason for that isolation is our broken, worthless selves.

I'm not trying to minimize the real mental illnesses regarding shame or isolation that people battle on a daily basis. There are God-gifted counselors who are capable of helping people who struggle with fear, anxiety, and shame, and there's nothing wrong with making use of them. In fact, after the accident, our amazing church, Bayside Community Church, and Pastor Randy Bezet provided a counselor that each member of the team could visit if we wanted to talk about things and get help dealing with the fall. I was reluctant at first, but about two weeks after the accident, I said to myself, *Okay, I'll go.* The psychologist was kind and polite, and after speaking with her and telling her my view on what happened (she'd already heard the story from several of the other members of the troupe), she said, "Well, you're going to have to deal with it."

I immediately replied, "Oh, I've dealt with it. I got back on the wire."

She pressed in on the fact that this wasn't enough—that I would need to really deal with the experience, but I didn't catch her meaning. I went to one session with her for about forty-five minutes, and then that was it. I never went back.

As I think about it now, I understand that she was right; I did have to deal with it, and despite what I thought at the time, I wasn't really addressing the deeper issue—mostly because I didn't know what that deeper issue was. I was looking at things from a purely factual perspective: I fell off a wire, I saw some of my dearest friends injured from the fall, and I was shaken. The only way to overcome the fear that spiraled out of that was to obviously get back on the wire again and remind myself that I could handle it. Despite being a person of faith, I didn't think about the supernatural perspective. I didn't consider that maybe this was a moment of spiritual warfare, and that's why the counseling route didn't work for me. But once I was aware of that reality, I put all of my focus on that arena. I was determined to conquer the Enemy who wanted to conquer me.

Not every personal battle is a spiritual one. But my battle was—my struggles with allowing a devastating visualization of the accident to go through my mind over and over again was more than just trauma. Beating myself up for no reason was more than just embarrassment. I needed to see the truth about what I was facing because it was the only way I was going to make progress. I needed to remember the truth I'd come to at the hospital: that God is sovereign, which meant that no matter what I was going through, he would make a way forward for me. It didn't mean everything was going to work out perfectly, but it did mean that things would work out for my good (Rom. 8:28). Once I remembered that God was in control of everything, I could turn my focus back to the second part of my belief: that I was in control of myself. I was in control of my thoughts, and I was in control of what I allowed to enter my mind, as well as what I allowed to come out of it.

It's not the pathway that everyone can walk, but it's the

one God placed before me, which meant it was time for me to start practicing what I'd always preached. Sitting there in my RV, I knew I had to do two things in order to make progress—first and foremost, I had to surrender the fears to God, and then I had to go to war within myself against the anxiety and cast out all of those fears. For too long, I'd been allowing the fear to make itself legitimate; I never questioned it when it came into my mind, never measured it against reality. Standing on the wire, shaking, I didn't stop and assess whether I was in any real danger—I just let the fear wash over me. I needed to go back to my training, which meant not allowing my fears to legitimize themselves.

That may sound a bit strange, so let me give you a little context. When I'm on the wire, I try to activate my faith at all times. I fully believe that I was made to do what I do, which means that when I'm walking on the wire, I'm pleasing God with every step. As a result, Satan would love nothing more than for me to *not* walk. While I have natural human responses to the danger in what I do—I'm a professional aerialist, but I'm not an idiot—I've found that the bigger battles are always in my mind. For instance, when I was walking over the Grand Canyon, there were forty-three-mile-an-hour wind gusts. My mind wanted to go crazy with fear because I was more than 1,500 feet up and out over the basin, far from either side, far from safety. But I countered that fear with the fact that I rehearsed with seventy-mile-an-hour winds; I'd literally trained for harsh gusts to assault me while I was over the canyon, so I was able to recenter myself on the truth that I was more than capable of safely making it across the wire. In fact, that is a perfect example of what I do—how I counter a negative thought with something positive that's related directly to that negative thought. I defeat fear with faith and facts.

It's why I train as hard and as specifically as I do. When I'm in the air, I need to be able to defeat the negative thoughts with the facts of my training. I don't just prepare for walking a wire, because I'm doing something greater than that. I know that people are watching me who not only will be inspired by what I'm doing but also will be curious as to how I do it with such confidence and skill. I've met people after Niagara Falls, the Grand Canyon, and so many other performances who wanted to know my secret for staying so calm and focused. And I always get to tell them about how I train and whom I walk to honor. It's one of the best things about what I do, and sitting in my RV, I knew in my heart I'd lost that.

Now I needed to get it back.

I needed to go back to basics, back to my training and my faith. Over the next days and weeks, every time I went into practice, I started thinking, *What do I tell myself to reaffirm that I'm okay up here?* Almost immediately, the options started flowing:

You've done this as much, if not more, than anyone in the world.

You've done it successfully.

You've probably done over a thousand seven-person pyramids with training and performances and had only one accident.

The odds are still on your side.

Those are the sorts of thoughts I used to convince

myself that I was okay. It didn't work right away, but I continued to do it. Whenever I began to visualize the accident, I would quickly visualize myself in the stands, watching the seven-person pyramid making it across and the audience being inspired, up on their feet cheering. Or I'd visualize myself standing on the far platform, the stunt complete, the team waving wildly to the crowd. I've found that visualizing what you want—really imagining the outcome you're chasing with detail and clarity—is an amazing way to overcome negative thoughts and feelings. We're visual learners, so it makes sense that a healthy picture in your mind can help you get a positive outcome.

It was a daily battle to think through that stuff, a mental discipline to keep the positive thoughts and truths ever present in my mind. As soon as the negative started to come, I'd cast it out, cast it out, cast it out—I'd practice my visualizations or review my training or remind myself that I was fully competent to complete the trick without a single error or misstep. It doesn't sound like much, but once I started practicing that over and over and over again, I was eventually able to make progress. I wasn't fully over the challenge—I would need another weapon in my arsenal, which I'll write about in the next chapter—but I was on my way toward a healthier attitude on the wire.

Whatever your struggle, whatever your need, there is a solution available to you. Maybe it's counseling; maybe it's learning to fight fear with facts; maybe it's learning to visualize the good outcome that you're working so desperately to achieve. Maybe, as it was for me, it's a wrestling of faith that will ultimately bring you peace. I don't know what you're facing, but I do know the world can overwhelm you, and I know there are probably days when you feel ashamed and alone. But you're not—you're surrounded by people who not only see you but know you and want the best for you. It can be difficult to see, but it doesn't change the truth that you have support that can help you stand strong. It doesn't change the truth that your life has a purpose and you're meant to fulfill it. Today may feel hopeless, but there's always hope. Work hard to make the best of today.

After all, making it one more day means making it one step closer to a better day.

CHAPTER 5

WORSHIP ON THE WIRE

THE ROAD TO OVERCOMING FEAR ISN'T A STRAIGHT line. When I started writing this chapter, I thought I knew where it was going to go. But then I was sitting in church listening to and singing the song "Stand in Your Love," by Josh Baldwin, which reminded me that when I'm standing in God's love, "my fear doesn't stand a chance."[1] I was overwhelmed with emotion. I broke into tears as this powerful thought came to mind: *The songs you sing have been prayers spoken over your entire life.*

It was an arresting moment, not only because I'm prone to emotional displays in church at least twice a month by the power of what is happening in a church service, but because this was such a powerful statement. So many people aren't prepared for the aftermath of their personal trauma or tragedy. The moment something unexpected or unfortunate happens in their lives, they are immediately adrift. That's how I felt after the accident—the world was still rolling on around me, but it sort of felt like I wasn't anchored to anything. I was floating through my days doing the best I knew to simply survive.

As I was working on this chapter, I came across an article from a book on trauma care, and it summed up some of the most common responses to a cataclysmic event:

> Initial reactions to trauma can include exhaustion, confusion, sadness, anxiety, agitation, numbness, dissociation, . . . physical arousal, and blunted affect. Most responses are normal in that they affect most survivors and are socially acceptable, psychologically effective, and self-limited.[2]

To say that knowledge would've been helpful on my journey is an understatement, and I think that's true for anyone experiencing the stress of a traumatic event. I've said for a long time that I didn't think I had PTSD, but I knew I was affected by what happened to me because I felt "off." Now I understand that I was experiencing the symptoms of stress after a trauma, which is different from PTSD—but more important, it is how the body naturally responds when things go wrong.

As I've been telling you my story, my goal has been to help you on your own journey. I've written as a guide, as someone who's walked the trail before you and can point out the major milestones along the way. In some ways, I've written as if this experience was in the past—but that moment in church made me realize it remains part of my present-day life. I'm no longer as affected as I was, but I'm by no means 100 percent over the accident. I'm not sure I ever will be.

Just after the church service that produced my epiphany, I was driving around with Erik Hedegaard, a reporter from *Rolling Stone* who was in town to interview me for a profile ahead of my walk over the Masaya volcano in Nicaragua. We were driving around Sarasota, sort of charting out my routine by exploring the places where I train and practice, when I drove through an intersection just around the corner from where the accident happened.

Almost instantly, I was caught up in a flashback. I was back in the ambulance with Lijana, sirens blaring, medics working to care for her, and I could see through the windshield that we were making a left-hand turn toward the hospital. I could smell the blood and the antiseptics they were using; the moment was *that* real to me. I teared up in the car because the feelings and thoughts were so overwhelming—much to the *Rolling Stone* reporter's dismay. I simply couldn't help myself; I immediately thought about my great-grandfather and how much deeper his pain must have been after the accident in Detroit. How he handled that kind of emotional gut punch is beyond me. I was fortunate that no one was killed in our accident, but sitting there at that red light, I felt genuine despair for how I would have handled everything if that hadn't been the case.

I share that to say that the aftermath of a life-changing event is inescapable. It permeates everything we do, and it goes with us everywhere. It's said that time heals every wound, but that doesn't mean the process will be easy or complete in my preferred timing. As a result, I'm still learning and growing from the challenges related to the accident, but I'm discovering that if I'm willing to dig in and address the fear, God is faithful to watch over me every step of the way.

So far I've talked a lot about my faith in the preceding chapters, and I'm going to continue sharing from that perspective now because it's essential to who I am. If you're reading this and you don't agree with my convictions, that's okay; you don't have to believe as I do to learn from what I'm about to offer. We all experience moments when we need to reach beyond ourselves for strength, and that transcendence is what often pulls us through the hardest times we face.

Whether we find that transcendence through worship, meditation, or a walk in the woods, the power we need to heal often comes from somewhere outside of ourselves, and I want to acknowledge that with this chapter.

MUSIC SOOTHES THE SAVAGE FEARS

As I wrote in the last chapter, my first step toward facing my fear was figuring out what I needed to do mentally. Between my conversations with Erendira and Dieter, I was breaking down the shame I felt, each conversation simultaneously allowing me to identify the problem. Once I clearly understood what was going on, I was ready to move forward. By acknowledging the reality of my situation, I could focus on my training, which in turn prompted me to work on getting my heart realigned with God.

When I talk about realignment, I'm not talking about

rededicating my life to Christ or even repenting of a specific sin. For me, it was returning to how I connected with God in my daily walk. I'm not a professional theologian, so I don't want to step into territory where my opinion might not be welcomed, but I will say this: I experience and connect with God most powerfully through music. Whenever I listen to worship songs, I feel the presence of God in my life in a way I don't experience with other forms. There's a great book by Richard Foster called *Celebration of Discipline* that lists several ways Christians have historically connected with and experienced God, and while certain forms like prayer, study, and fasting are more commonly known, worship is one that Foster highlights, calling it "our human response to God's divine initiative."[3]

In recent years, I've put worship songs on repeat, leaning into this practice in a way I hadn't before. It became clear to me that listening to the music was a way of praying—of allowing words of peace and victory to wash over me. That may sound strange to you, especially if I were to walk up to you on the street and ask you to define the word *prayer*. I think most people, religious or not, would say it's something along the lines of "talking to God" or "a conversation with Jesus," and those answers wouldn't be wrong.

They also wouldn't be enough.

Prayer is worship, worship is prayer, and it took the aftermath of the accident for me to really connect those dots. Whenever I'm on a wire now, I play my playlist and consider it praying. Once the music starts, my mind is stilled, my heart finds its rhythm, and I feel at home in the world.

If that sounds strange to you, it's okay. Not everyone understands the feeling I'm trying to describe; there's a definite otherworldly quality to the sensation of knowing you're pleasing God with literally every step you take. I've spoken to other performers whose faiths are important to them— both in my line of work and in others—and I've heard a handful talk about the same thing. When they are playing their music or making their art, they have an overwhelming sense of how happy God is with them in that moment. I've met nonperformers—parents, grandparents, the occasional businessperson—who've said similar things, but there might be something particular to the performance crowd that makes the feeling I'm talking about a little more concrete. They get what I'm trying to say.

As I've said, I feel like God connects with me most powerfully through music. I've gravitated toward worship songs ever since I was a little kid. As early as when I was three, I was instantly transfixed by music whenever I heard it. In the car, my mom used to play these cassettes called *Kids' Praise!* by Psalty the Singing Songbook. They were worship songs for kids, and I remember wearing out those tapes when I was younger. Eventually, Mom swapped them out for Christian artists like Keith Green and Phil Driscoll, but no matter what she played, music remained a conduit for me to understand and encounter God.

It's not just Christian music, though that's primarily what I listen to. I remember being in church one day, and the worship team opened with a song that was popular on the local pop station at the time, "Unwell" by Matchbox Twenty. It has a bit of a folksy flavor to it, but what arrested me were the lyrics, which talked about how the songwriter wasn't crazy, just a little unwell—even if other people couldn't tell the difference. I was especially moved by the way the lyrics spoke of the challenges of other people perceiving someone's pain through a lens of judgment. I am a compassionate person, and sometimes when I hear a song that speaks to the struggles other people face or struggles that I can identify in my own life, I'm overcome with emotion. It's a way of tapping into the deepest part of myself and letting God stir my soul.

A number of the songs on my playlist have at least one verse or chorus that deals with fear and overcoming it. I didn't plan it that way; I chose the songs because they moved me as a whole, not just because they mentioned victory over fear. Chances are I would've actually tried to avoid them if I'd realized the common theme—I didn't want to be reminded that I was afraid. I wanted the opposite feeling; I wanted to feel empowered. Strengthened. I wanted a sense that God was greater than my fear. One of the songs that came to mind often was "Surrounded (Fight My Battles)" by Michael W. Smith. The lyrics are simple and repetitive, but they spoke to me and gave me strength as I learned how to fight my battles: when it feels like I'm surrounded, I just have to remember that I'm surrounded by God.

When you're fighting for control of your own heart and mind, you don't necessarily need the most complex lyrics. You need something that speaks truth and peace and can keep you focused on both. The best songs are the ones that communicate the truth of God; the lyrics are not necessarily direct quotes from Scripture, but they have a lot of Scripture in them. I had plenty of these songs in my playlist:

"Stand in Your Love"—Josh Baldwin and Bethel Music
"You Make Me Brave"—Amanda Cook and Bethel Music
"Good, Good Father"—Chris Tomlin
"Behold"—Hillsong Worship
"Mighty to Save"—Hillsong Worship
"This I Believe"—Hillsong Worship
"Clean"—Natalie Grant
"Jesus"—Chris Tomlin
"Do It Again"—Elevation Worship

When I look back at my playlist now, one song really stands out: "No Longer Slaves" by Bethel Music featuring Jonathan David and Melissa Helser. The chorus simply repeats, "I am no longer a slave to fear / I am a child of God!"[4] I mean, you couldn't possibly get more on the nose than that, and yet those exact words weren't what connected most with me at the time. It was the entire song, the whole work, that gave me strength when I listened to it. I was letting those words sink into my mind and my heart, absorbing them without processing them, but taking them in so they would be a constant prayer over me day after day, no matter how I was feeling. On days when I felt scared, I'd quote a lyric. On days when I had doubts, I'd sing a verse or two of something upbeat. If I worried about shaking or falling or just being out of control in general, I'd grab my earbuds, open my playlist, and let the song say what I couldn't. I'd let the artists pray over me when I couldn't pray over myself.

I'm reminded of when Satan was testing Jesus in the wilderness. This was before Jesus began preaching and teaching all over Israel; he was in the desert, and the Bible says that he'd been fasting for forty days. Now, I don't know if you've ever tried fasting, but three days is long enough for me to feel run-down and weak. After forty days, I imagine Jesus was beyond himself and very vulnerable—which is probably why Satan came to him then. He loves to hit people when they're weakest.

Satan said to Jesus something like, "If you're so hungry, why don't you just turn one of these rocks into bread? Surely you have the power to do that." Jesus answered him with scripture: "It is written: 'Man shall not live on bread alone, but on every word that comes from the mouth of God'" (Matt. 4:4). Two more times Satan tempted Jesus—once to reveal his divine connection with God, and once to worship Satan and be given all power on earth. Each time, Jesus replied with a quote from the Bible. It strikes me that even in his weakest moments, the words Jesus likely had learned when he was a child came to his rescue.

That's the way it is for me with praise music: the words that I've been hearing since I was a child, the words I continue to pour over my life today, are prayers that fight for me when I don't know how to fight for myself. When I'm weak, those words give me strength. When I'm lost, they give me direction. When I need encouragement, they pick me up. When I need clarity, they provide focus, and when

I need to overcome fear, they remind me that God is bigger than any fear I might have.

Maybe you have something like that in your own life. If you're a person of faith, maybe you find that connection through prayer or hearing a good sermon. Or maybe you're not religious at all but have a certain beach or place in the mountains you go to when you feel like giving up. For me, when I'm listening to good music, I know that God is with me. It goes beyond words, too—I'm moved not only by the lyrics but also by the way the music and words work together to tap into hidden emotions and thoughts that I don't know how to express in other ways.

For as much as I love music, you would think that I'm a good singer. But funny enough, I'm not. I'm truly in the category of "make a joyful noise," but it doesn't diminish the experience for me at all. I'll happily stand in the middle of a crowded church or stadium and let the music and the words and the voices wash over me. When that happens, I find peace in God.

That's why I listen to praise music when I walk the wire—every time. It soothes me, takes away the nerves and the anxiety, and keeps me connected to God in a way that gives me power. I know when I'm walking, there's a chance someone down below is wondering, *How does he do that?* My desire is that I would be so in tune with God that it would be obvious that supernatural power aids me across the wire. Interestingly, I don't have worship music on during any pyramid wire act, but I do for almost all of my solo walks. But when I've got music in my ears, I feel as though my feet are stepping onto solid ground even as I'm hundreds of feet in the air.

Maybe it would work for you too.

THE POWER OF SONG

While thinking through this chapter, I attempted to learn more about why music is so helpful to me when I walk. I'm more than happy to stop with the spiritual answer—that it's how God meets with me—yet as I mentioned earlier, I know not everyone is religious. But that doesn't mean the idea of music helping you past your fears doesn't hold merit for you. In fact, according to science, it might be a key to helping you, even more than you realize.

Frontiers in Psychology is an online journal where you can access lots of papers written by qualified researchers and practitioners in the field. I was looking for something that not only explained the way music affected my brain but might also help someone who isn't particularly religious. I found an article by seven different researchers that was a revelation for me. The basic idea of the paper was that music is a "potent mood regulator that can induce relaxation and reduce anxiety in different situations."[5] That's good news in and of itself, but the way they came to their conclusion is what fascinated me.

The researchers set up an experiment that would induce people's *fear of heights*, then tested to see how music helped them.

I couldn't pass that up! While my fear wasn't a fear of heights per se, it was the fear of what happened from a fall. I dug into the research and found that the scientists had their subjects put on virtual reality goggles, which simulated an elevator ride up the outside of a 106-story building. Forty participants were selected from a group of people who responded to an email sent to their university campus. Researchers gave each person something called an "Acrophobia Questionnaire," which measures fear of heights. The participants had to be around eighteen years of age, and their responses had to range from no fear of heights to being petrified of them so the results would have a good mix. The scientists measured heart rate, skin response, balance, and head movements during the simulation, and then they measured each person's experience of anxiety using a series of three questionnaires.[6]

They separated the participants into two groups: one group experienced the "elevator ride" with background music; the other experienced the ride without it. What they found was a significant increase in stress both objectively (through the measurements of heart rate, skin response, and so on) and subjectively in the group that experienced the ride *without* music. As a result, they concluded that "music can to some extent facilitate post-stress recovery."[7]

Keep in mind that the music wasn't chosen by the participants. It had little to no personal meaning for the people in the study—it was literally just elevator music being piped into a fake digital elevator ride. And yet there was still something comforting about it! Now imagine the difference it would have made if every participant could've selected their favorite song or a song that had meaning to them. It's not a scientific conclusion, but it's an easy one to draw: chances are pretty good those folks would've felt even better.

Maybe music doesn't help calm you down or give you a connection to a power greater than yourself. Maybe you need to go for a run or play some golf or write a poem. Maybe you need to take slow drives through the country or spend time relaxing in a bath. Whatever your mechanism, you have tools at your disposal that can help you connect with the rest of yourself, beyond your conscious, walking-around mind, and those tools can be used to help you heal.

That's my bigger point: use the tools you have to help you get better. My greatest tool is music because it helps me find the power that's bigger than me; it helps me connect to the God of the universe who made everything and knows everything and holds everything—including my life—in his capable hands. That's where I find my peace, in the truth of God's existence, and it was something I lost after the accident in Sarasota. Once I got back to it, I began to notice a change, an increased confidence and a decreased stress level. I was able to tap back into my empathy and compassion for other people and rediscover my desire to use my work as a way to help people know God exists. I began to walk around the arena and pray for the people who would come see us perform, thanking God for their lives and praising him for my opportunity to do what I do for a living.

In short, I became myself again.

There were still days when I had to battle the fear and the anxiety, or just wrestle with being tired and weak. I'm not superhuman. I don't heal faster than anyone else. But now that I know how to chase after my healing, things are different for me, and the spiritual component plays an important part—which is why I wrote this chapter.

Do whatever you need to do to restore your soul. Chase God. Chase waves. Climb a tree. Eat a great meal. Just make sure that while you're working so hard with your mind to process what is going on in your life, you also work on your soul. Once you remember to care for your soul, you rediscover who you are and where your strength is, and that's what it takes to continue the journey toward healing.

It wasn't long after I had this breakthrough that I began to have thoughts about redeeming the accident. It was a mark on my family's name and a black mark in my life, but it wasn't beyond being redeemed by God. I knew another pyramid act wouldn't cut it—I was already doing that in Atlantic City; and anyway, what I wrestled with wasn't a need for redemption for myself. I had made my turn toward wholeness, and I would continue to walk that path. Instead, my mind pulled up someone else's face, someone else who would need restoration in a way that would be long and hard and challenging. Someone who would need my help in more ways than one. I began thinking and dreaming and praying of the day when Lijana would walk a wire again. She just had to get past the hospital first and then go to work on overcoming her fear, just as I had overcome my own.

And she would have me by her side to help her do just that.

CHAPTER 6

THE ROAD TO RECOVERY

LIJANA'S JOURNEY BACK FROM THE ACCIDENT IS WOR-thy of its own book. After the Big Apple Circus, I came back to Sarasota and put my focus on helping her recover. My sister is tremendously strong—her ability to bounce back from her injuries is nothing short of inspiring because she had to rehabilitate her body, mind, and spirit. It was a much harder and more difficult journey than I can even begin to describe.

The guilt and emotional stress I had been feeling for allowing my sister to get injured was only magnified because of something I haven't told you yet: Lijana wouldn't have been on the wire if not for a last-minute team choice. You see, we didn't ask her originally because she was busy performing with her own wire team in Las Vegas, but a week before the Sarasota show was set to open, the person we had originally chosen backed out. We needed a pinch hit-ter, someone we could trust implicitly and wouldn't have to spend a ton of time training. We needed a pro, and we needed that person quickly.

We needed Lijana.

Lijana has wire walking in her blood just like I do. I can remember when we were kids out in our backyard practicing together, her helping me, me helping her, the two of us speaking the unspoken language of a family that lives for the same passion. She'd also held the pyramid with me before, so I knew we could bring Lijana in, even with only a week of training, and our bond would be able to cut through the time pressure.

Other people have done an eight-person pyramid before, but the top level of the pyramid is just two people together, instead of building to a true point. So it's essentially four people on the bottom, two in the middle, and two up top. In my mind, this could be seen as cutting corners. Sure, it provides for more stability, but it doesn't give the audience the same *Wow!* as a true pyramid structure: four people as the base, two people as the second level, one person as the third level—and the final person sitting atop their shoulders as the top. That's what we do, and it's dangerous.

The highest we'd ever done it was twenty-five feet off the ground in Japan, which set a world record in 2001. We'd be attempting to break that record in Sarasota by raising the wire to twenty-eight feet, so we needed someone who could handle the pressure—which is what caused our original teammate to back out. As the front person of the second level, he was the one who had to hold his balance so the third and top levels could hold theirs. He was still a bit shaky, even after all the rehearsals, and he simply couldn't handle the stress.

We could still do the seven-person pyramid and be within our contract. But we didn't want to miss the opportunity to do the eight-person again, this time in front of our friends and family, on our home soil. As I've written before, my vision for our family's legacy is to elevate the general public's perception of circus performances, and holding a world-record eight-person pyramid for the opening night of Sarasota would be an example of how we go beyond everyone's expectations and deliver to the greatest of our ability. So even though we didn't have to call Lijana, even though we could've settled for the seven and kept our contract intact, we knew it wouldn't be a record. Plus, we would know that we delivered less than what was possible, and we were not willing to settle for that.

So I called Lijana and asked, "Do you want to be a part of this?"

"Heck yeah, I do," she replied, "but let me practice holding a few pyramids with 250 pounds on my shoulders down low here in Vegas and send you guys a video to see what your team thinks." Later that day we received a video of Lijana practicing and watched it as a team. We all agreed to have her jump on the next plane cross-country.

That's the way it is with with Lijana and me—we're willing to be there for each other, to be part of anything the other one is doing. Lijana told me she was willing to do anything we needed her to do, and that's what she did. With less than a week to go, she came in and took the same place she held back in 2001, the second-level spot of the pyramid. She jumped into rehearsals with the team and even practiced a lot by herself by carrying heavy weights on her shoulders. Her work ethic was unstoppable, and despite the time crunch and Lijana's learning curve, everything was going well. We practiced the eight-person several times in the first five days after her arrival, and she gave us nothing less than her best.

Each practice saw us get a little bit better as a team; the night before the accident, we took the pyramid up to twenty-eight feet, and it went well. It wasn't perfect, mind you, but it was good, so we called it a night and went to dinner and laughed for hours, talking about how much we were enjoying being together.

The next day, we came in for the final dress rehearsal. I knew there were still a lot of nerves, and not just the typical opening-night jitters. We were attempting an eight-person pyramid at a world-record height, and we were doing it with a team member who had only been with us less than a week. Just like every time we perform the seven- or eight-person pyramid, I checked in with every member of the team moments before we began to build the pyramid.

"How you feeling? Good?"

"Good!"

"Good. Okay, let's go."

And we began. As we were walking out on the wire, I remember that everything was going smooth at first, but then things changed probably eight steps out, which is about where I stopped. I saw a balancing pole swing way down, and I thought, *Something's not right.* And then the pyramid just toppled before I could say anything.

LOOKING AHEAD, NOT BEHIND

During the aftermath of the fall, I saw a guy videotaping with his phone, and it enraged me. I remember thinking, *What kind of sicko would video my family bleeding in the ring?* One of my friends went up and grabbed the phone from him. This wasn't something any of us wanted to have around to bring back horrific memories. I understand if that sounds extreme to you, but here's why I felt so strongly: I didn't want any of my family to be able to relive the accident. Of course, we live in an age of cameras and screens, so being filmed is now the norm. I learned from the police report that they acquired the video of the accident from his phone because the police wanted to see if there were grounds for criminal charges, if any foul play was involved. The police investigation was different from the OSHA investigation, which assessed whether the accident was the result of a rigging failure or something wrong that we did within the work space. They cleared us immediately.

About a month later, after Lijana was released from the hospital, my fear about the video footage going public became the focus of an important conversation. Despite the severity of her injuries, Lijana was out relatively quickly, and we were able to get the entire team together at a restaurant in Sarasota called Gecko's. We met in a private room—with

Andrew, Rietta, and Lijana all in wheelchairs—so we could have the chance to talk in peace.

After we greeted one another and there was a pause in the conversation, I said, "I've learned that there's a video out of the accident."

Everyone looked at me, stone-faced. No one said a word. I looked each person in the eyes: Blake, Andrew, Nick, Zeb, Rietta, Alec, and, finally, Lijana.

"I don't ever want to see that video," I said. "It's bad enough I have to see flashes of it in my mind. I don't need to see it in real life."

We then went around the table, discussing the pros and cons, and decided as a group that we wouldn't watch it. We were grateful to have survived—we would move forward from the accident, not look back. Everyone, as a group, agreed that it would be best to not ever see the video. We then made a pact, a promise to one another, as a sign of solidarity and a strong bond of an inseparable team.

It's been more than three years since we made that pact, and despite all of the television appearances I've done where they play clips from the video, I've still never watched it. I know that it's on YouTube and has been shared on countless news sites, but whenever I'm around and it's on a screen, I close my eyes, turn my head, or leave the room. The visual would simply be too powerful in my mind, and I don't need that kind of competition inside my brain—not to mention that I made a promise to my team, and I am a man of my word. I need to be able to walk out on the line with a clear head every single time.

I know others in the group have since decided that watching the video was right for them and their healing, and while I'm disappointed that they went back on their word, I know that each of us has had to do what we believed was right. For me, keeping my mind free from disturbing images is what I must do to stay healthy. And healthy is what matters.

Lijana's injuries healed as time went by, and she was able to begin rehab. The swelling and pain in her face subsided, and soon enough she was back on her feet. What she wasn't back on, however, was a wire. Unlike me, Lijana didn't go right back to performing. She's an amazing coach, with a high-wire troupe that she's been instructing for years. She threw herself back into her coaching and spent her time investing in them, helping them grow from her experience. I couldn't blame her after all she went through. Because of the fall, she spent weeks in the hospital and months in pain, working to get back to the person she was before the accident. Her journey was hers to make. She was alive, and she was well, and she was my sister, and those three things meant more to me than anything else. Lijana's recovery was all that mattered, and my responsibility was to support her, cheer her on, and be her brother—even if she never walked on a wire again.

So while she got better, I got busy booking new events and picking up more opportunities to deliver speeches to companies, which was a goal of mine. The months passed, and 2017 became 2018. In the middle of 2018, I challenged my manager to help me land another big event. I wanted to do something that would really capture people's attention.

I wanted to pursue a walk in New York City between two skyscrapers, and my manager proposed Times Square.

A HEALING OPPORTUNITY

I hadn't been in the city for an event since Erendira and I performed there with Big Apple Circus. I imagined it would be pretty awesome being suspended above such an iconic city, looking at the skyline that you normally can only see in a photo. I really liked the idea of a walk over NYC, but I wanted to go higher and longer than Times Square and felt that walk wouldn't be an exciting enough special on its own, simply because of what I'd done in the past. For TV viewers, how does a 250-foot-high walk over a crowded city compare to Niagara Falls or the Grand Canyon? In my mind it couldn't, which is why I initially didn't want to do it.

So I began to focus on creating something magical for the TV audience, but I didn't quite know what that was until I hopped on the plane heading back to Sarasota. It was then that I realized the answer to the problem. I was listening to worship music, and I was praying. Looking out of the window, I whispered, "God, I don't know what to do here. I really don't know. I don't feel like this is enough. It's not big enough, exciting enough, dramatic enough. But what would be?"

Then, it dawned on me. The thought came into my mind and literally made me sit up.

You should do this walk with your sister.

I stared out at the clouds, and the thought continued.

She's the one who's overcoming such a traumatic event. This will be an incredible opportunity for her. It's redemption. It's everything that she needs.

Having made my own journey toward healing by getting back on the wire, I naturally felt like this was a wonderful idea. After all, Lijana and I grew up the same—we had the same passion, the same love of the wire, the same desire to perform—so it made sense that our full healing could be found the same way. But my enthusiasm was tripped up by one single thought: she had gotten hurt, not me. Maybe her pathway couldn't be like mine. Maybe it would have to be some other way. The guilt rose up in me for a moment; after all, she'd only fallen because I'd asked her to walk with us. But my faith rose up to fight that guilt. It reminded me that God had taken care of Lijana and everyone on the wire. There were injuries, yes, but everyone had lived. I thought about something the doctor told me the first day Lijana was in the hospital: of the five people who fell from the wire, statistically two of them should've died based on the height of the fall. We'd beaten the odds on the front end of the accident, so who was to say we couldn't beat them again on the back end?

I believed that Lijana could find healing by getting back on a wire. But did Lijana?

CHAPTER 7

WALKING TOWARD HEALING

WHEN I WAS GROWING UP, MY FAMILY HAD A SMALL wire strung across our backyard. It's the one I first walked when I was two. It's the one my mother and father patiently instructed me on, teaching me the mechanics and movements of the Wallenda family. I remember falling off that wire and landing in the grass. I remember my first turn on that wire. I remember the first time I sat down on that wire. But more than anything else, what I remember about that wire is that almost any time I was on it, so was Lijana. We would pretend we were our mom and dad or that we were in their act. Being on the wire together was as natural for us as being together anywhere else.

With New York firmly in mind, I was thinking about that backyard wire a lot in the days before I finally called her to pitch the idea. I was hoping that what we shared was more than a last name, more than just good memories. I was hoping we shared that same drive to be on the wire again.

Finally, I called her.

When she answered, I didn't waste a second. I simply said, "Lijana, would you consider doing a walk across Times Square with me?"

There was a pause, and it was scary for me, nerve-racking even, because I was talking to somebody who had fallen from a wire twenty-eight feet in the air. (It was more like thirty-eight feet, since she was on that second level.) And not only that, but she was still recovering, still rehabbing, still going through surgeries to get back to herself. I just didn't know what she would say.

"Absolutely" was her response. "I want to do it."

She began telling me how she'd been slowly getting back on the wire, as much as her injuries would allow. She started out low, like maybe twenty-four inches off the ground, but she was gradually increasing the height as much and as often as she could because, in her words, "I was born for this."

That was all I needed to hear. After we talked, I called my manager and told him that Lijana was in—Times Square was a go. It didn't take long for our broadcast partners to sign on to the idea, and we quickly arrived at a date: June 23, 2019. We would string a 1,250-foot-long cable—three times longer than anything Lijana had walked before—from the roof of 1 Times Square to the roof of 2 Times Square. We would be twenty-five stories in the air (250 feet) and the cable would have a twelve degree incline from one end to the other. I would start on the higher end and walk downhill toward Lijana, who would start on the lower end. We would meet in the middle, she would sit down, I would step over her, she would get back up, and then we would walk to our respective rooftop endpoints. All live on television, with an audience cheering below in Times Square. Meanwhile, as we walked, the television announcers would share Lijana's incredible story of recovery and tell the world about our walk to redemption. There would be press, media appearances, and lots of opportunities for us to talk about what God did in our lives after the accident. I was excited thinking about it because I knew it would be incredible.

I also knew the production was going to be a challenge because I was going to have to pull double duty: I would not only serve as executive producer for the walk but also have to help coach Lijana for the stunt. I didn't think either job individually would be especially challenging—certainly nothing I hadn't handled before—but the idea of splitting my attention made me a little nervous. I didn't want to underserve either of those roles, especially with Lijana. She was putting her faith in me again, and after Sarasota, I was not going to let her down. I was going to do everything in my power to make sure she not only *felt* safe but actually *was* safe. She nearly lost her life trusting me once; now here she was trusting again. God forbid that something would happen this time. I'm not sure I could have lived with myself.

There were days the pressure felt overwhelming, but I couldn't show it. Ironically, one of the first things we would have to address was the safety harness that New York state law requires performers to wear. It was going to be an issue.

REBUILDING TRUST

Our family preference is not to use safety lines, but the good people of the state of New York and my TV network partner felt differently, maybe because so many daredevils careened over the edge of Niagara Falls in barrels. When I performed my walk across the falls in 2012, I not only had to have safety equipment to make the crossing, but the governor also had to sign legislation giving me permission. The legal hoops were easy enough to navigate, but helping Lijana get accustomed to the safety harness would take some work. And we would have to figure out how to complete our walk in light of the fact that the harnesses would make it almost impossible for Lijana and me to cross over at the center of the wire. My brain was turning nonstop for a solution.

Safety harnesses aside, there was also the issue of the event being bigger than anything Lijana had ever done before. My sister is an accomplished performer and has done some amazing things with her troupe performing at Absinthe in Las Vegas. But the size of the stunt I was proposing was going to be a significant challenge. It was farther and higher than she'd ever walked before, and we were going to completely stop our momentum in the middle of the wire in order to execute the cross. Oh, and we had to contend with the wire being on an incline. It was enough to scare a seasoned solo performer who'd never had anything go wrong, but throw in the two of us, the accident, and the watching eyes of a world that can't wait to see if you fail, and it was a big hill to climb.

And that's really the only reason I agreed to do the walk.

The challenge of wanting to be great and pursue great-ness rests in answering this central question: *How do you continue to grow?* How do you find your next win? How do you step outside of your comfort zone? In traditional sports, you move from game to game, from opponent to opponent; in business, you tackle the next problem your customer faces. But when you do what we do for a living, growth isn't marked by making more money. It's not about being an MVP or winning the championships. Instead, it's all about facing and conquering mental and physical chal-lenges that could hurt or even kill you. Candidly, it's one thing to say that when you've never really been hurt by the wire. But coming off of Sarasota, seeing how hard and how long Lijana had to work just to get back to normal, the sensation changed. I understood that our walk across Times Square, as cool as it would be, was truly a testimony to something deeper, more significant, more powerful than the average person dreams about. It was a shout to the world that God, the one we worship and who made each person on this planet with care and love, was firmly in control.

We would demonstrate this by being in control of our-selves. I knew that Lijana and I would have to train for this like nothing else we'd ever done. I would have to push her limits, and mine, to get us fully prepared for whatever might happen on the wire. We would train in Sarasota, and we would train hard, incorporating elements I'd used for my walks across Niagara Falls and the Grand Canyon. We'd have simulated wind; we'd have simulated rain; we would walk across a variety of wires in order to find our strength and balance no matter what the wire might do or how it might feel. We would go back to the Wallenda way: *put your feet on the wire right, hold tight to the pole, never lose your cool, and you will never fail.*

I knew the first thing I would have to do is get Lijana re-accustomed to the wire. Though she'd been walking some at her home in Las Vegas, I knew that she was more confident in the wire than in herself, and that wasn't where I needed her to be. I needed her to be assured of her own abilities, her own strengths. The wire that we were going to walk across Times Square was going to be the safest, most secure wire she'd ever walked, but if she had any doubts about her ability or her strength, the wire wouldn't matter. She could potentially fall. We had to remove that potential. So I strung up a low-hanging wire in my backyard, not unlike the one we grew up walking, but I made it as sloppy and wobbly a wire as possible. The first time she stepped on it, she looked at me as if I were crazy.

"This isn't very secure, Nik."

"I know—but try it anyway."

She did try it, and watching her wobble around, searching to find herself and her footing, was hard. I didn't want to see her bail on the wire, even if it was only three feet off the ground. I wanted her to stick with it and prove that she could recover. The first day she walked only fifty feet or so of the eight-hundred-foot-long training wire, and it really freaked her out. It was like no wire she had ever walked on before because I had intentionally made it incredibly unstable. It took her more than a week to build up enough courage to walk the entire length. Even then she was still walking very slowly and cautiously. It was as much of a mental battle as a physical battle.

After about ten days, we began to talk through the routine and how it would go. I told her the wire would have a little bit of movement because of the height and because I would be walking toward her.

She looked at me the way only an older sibling can. "I'm not stupid, Nik."

"I know. I just don't want to take anything for granted. I don't want anything to happen to you."

"What about you?"

"Or me. But if anything were to happen to you, it would be as if it were happening to me. I don't want to live through that again."

After that, I continued to string up sloppy lines at increasing heights. We went from three feet to five; from five to ten; from ten to twenty. It was around thirty-five feet that we began to simulate wind conditions, bringing in fans that would blow at varying speeds. We got up to as high as fifty miles per hour during some of our sessions. That's a ridiculous speed, I know, but the wind cuts through the New York buildings in ways that can really mess you up. One big gust and you could be off the wire, the walk over in more ways than one. We threw in rain simulations, too—anything to make us constantly focus and refocus on what our bodies were doing at every moment. We wanted to make sure that we were so locked in on our job of walking from building to building that crossing over in the middle would be a minor inconvenience on the way to our goal.

In some ways, it was like being a child again. Working with Lijana and getting the chance to reconnect after the accident was a blessing—and it brought to life one blessing

I didn't expect. If you've ever been through a traumatic event, you know what I'm talking about: it gets easy to be with people without being *with* them. You can be present yet distant, connected yet removed. I hadn't been aware of feeling any of that with Lijana, but it surfaced as we practiced for hours every day. I began to realize how much I had pulled away in the aftermath of the accident. Maybe it was part of the shame I struggled with, or maybe it was just because she had to work so hard on her recovery. As I watched her working, I realized that although each of us had recovered from the fall, we were both still healing, and there was a difference between the two.

Recovery means getting back to how you used to feel. Healing means getting used to how you are now. Some people call it embracing the new normal, but whatever you call it, it requires work and dedication, and Lijana and I were doing all of that together as we rehearsed.

INCHING OUR WAY TO NEW YORK

When I wasn't walking the wire with Lijana, I was on the phone with our production partners, making sure that everything in New York was coming together. There were site visits to make, measurements to take, legal documents to sign, marketing to create, press to book, and a thousand other things that needed my near-constant attention. In a way, it was my own form of a "sloppy wire"—I had to fight to get my head in the game every time Lijana and I were together. I had to learn to trust myself again. To aid me, I made a playlist of new worship songs and shared it with Lijana. We don't always have the same tastes, but she enjoyed the songs I shared with her, as they gave us a common focus on the wire. We both decided that when we walked in New York, we'd wear our earbuds so we could not only listen to the same playlist but have the ability to communicate with each other as well.

As we came through the winter into the spring, Lijana and I added media appearances to our routine. We were still practicing each day, but we began talking to various media outlets around the country, both print and television. We did local news in Florida and made our way to some of the talk shows around the country. Each place we went, we talked about the redemption we were seeking. It's funny, but I've mentioned how I've always sought to redeem things that my family had done—the fall in Detroit, my great-grandfather's fall in Puerto Rico—but redeeming the past felt different from what Lijana and I were chasing. We weren't seeking to redeem the fall in Sarasota; we were seeking to redeem ourselves from what the Enemy wanted to bring out of the fall. We were rebuilding the final pieces of our faith.

Soon enough, we were in the middle of May, and it was time to begin working on the set for the walk. My team and I would do the rigging, and as always, I asked my father, Terry, to oversee everything. I always want his eyes on each piece of the rig, from the smallest bolt to the wire itself, because I want his blessing and experienced assurance that everything is rigged safely and properly. In fact, I had gone to him and Mom and asked for their okay before I even spoke to Lijana, and well before I signed off on the walk.

Those final days were tremendously stressful. The distance and the incline proved to be significantly more challenging than Lijana and I anticipated, so the rigging process kept changing. This caused a lot of concern for both of us. Just days before the walk, Lijana came to me with some doubt, and I promised her we would get it right, that everything would work out. But she wasn't sure—and neither was I. What was our private struggle became public the Thursday before the walk when *ABC News* and other outlets reported on the problems we were experiencing. In the end, the report only served to drive up the drama for our Sunday walk, which meant the viewership was going to be up. That same day, I appeared on *Good Morning America* and took Michael Strahan up to the platforms where we would walk. That morning there was a thick fog in the city, which made visibility challenging. Strahan asked me if I was scared.

"It's a little intimidating," I said.

"What do you mean?" Strahan asked.

"One of the challenges that we have," I said, pointing to the platform, "is we're at 17 stories here"—I pointed to the opposite platform—"but we're at 25 stories there. . . . It's pretty steep on that end, a little more than I expected . . . so it's stressful for me. I have to walk down that incline so it's extremely intimidating for me just standing up here looking at it."[1]

The rest of that weekend is a blur. There were so many details that needed attending to, so many commitments that required my time. By the time Sunday rolled around, I was just grateful for show day.

SHOWTIME

Lijana and I met beforehand, and we prayed together for strength and courage. I was nervous—I will admit I wasn't sure if she would be able to step out onto the wire, let alone walk it all the way. For all that we'd practiced, there was no way to practice the courage needed in the moment. You simply can't replicate it. It's either in you or it isn't.

I made my way to my platform, twenty-five stories up, and the crew helped me into my safety harness. There were crew members of all types: television crew, production crew, rigging crew, people who were there to make sure nothing went wrong, and people who were there in case something *did* go wrong. I knew there was just as much commotion on Lijana's side, but I couldn't help her beyond what I'd done, and I wondered if what I'd done was enough. I wouldn't fully know until I stepped out on the wire and began my walk.

Once everything was set up and checked for safety, the countdown to the broadcast began. Strahan was serving as a host from the top of the skyscraper Lijana started on and was connected into my in-ear monitor to tell me when to take my first steps. There were cameras positioned all along the wire's span, above and below, and on the platforms as well. Whatever happened to Lijana and me, there was no way anyone could miss it. I laughed to myself as I thought about the person who'd videotaped the fall in Sarasota with his phone. I was mad at that camera, but now I was about to welcome in tens of thousands of cell phones with no more control over what was about to happen than I'd had in Sarasota. It's funny how life does that. It was just one more thing God could redeem.

When Strahan gave me the word, I took a careful step onto the wire and got my pole in position. The playlist began to play in my ear. With worship ringing in my ears, and a peace filling my heart, I began my steady descent toward the middle of the wire, hoping that Lijana would meet me there. I purposely started before Lijana so that I could report back to her on how the wire felt. I could also report to my team in case they needed to make any last-second adjustments before she started walking out. It didn't take long for me to tell her that the wire felt firm and steady and to let her know that it was safe to start her trek. We would meet exactly where we should on the wire and begin the delicate crossover dance.

The incline of the wire was unnoticeable because I was so focused on Lijana and her safety. I also knew that it wouldn't be as stressful on her going up the incline, because she wouldn't be fighting gravity. We made our way to the rendezvous point quickly, and as I approached her, Lijana began positioning herself to sit down. I was going to reach down and unhook her safety harness—a move that we'd been able to get approved—and then step over her. I would then reach back, reattach the harness, and make sure she was steady as she stood back up. Of everything we would do on the wire that night, the crossover was the most difficult.

I concentrated on the music in my ears as Lijana sat down on the wire and hooked herself directly in, and I was feeling good as I moved to disconnect her harness. But then terror struck: my balancing pole started to slide down. My grip had slipped just slightly, and I felt my breath catch.

Lijana looked up at me. "Are you okay, Nik?"

Her eyes helped me come back to myself. I stepped over her and reached back, being sure to keep my pole balanced; then I reattached the safety line to her. I held my breath before she stood back to her feet; after what I'd just experienced, I was suddenly worried she would struggle to stand. That worry grew when her balance pole became entangled in its own tether. But Lijana unclipped it and got it reattached, and then I heard her say behind me, "In Jesus' name, I've got this. In Jesus' name. Thank you, Lord." She stood again, to great applause from far below, and was back on her way. With that we both continued walking the last leg of our respective journeys. I was able to complete my walk quickly, which meant I had time to get off the wire and watch Lijana.

I hustled my way down to the street and looked up; she was taking her time as she navigated the final length of the wire. I marveled at her courage and strength as she faced her fear. Each of us has to face our fears at our own pace, and I got to watch her take those last few steps. The hair on my arms stood up, and I raced my way to her building, hurrying to the top so I could be there when the crew reached out and helped her step to safety. Once she was on the platform, we embraced, squeezing each other tightly. I got goose bumps then, and I have them now just thinking about that moment. It was life-changing for us both.

Two years after the fall, I had helped my sister heal. And she had done the same for me.

CHAPTER 8

FEAR OF FEATHERS

UP UNTIL THIS POINT, I'VE SHARED ABOUT MY STORY AND how I've been able to overcome a very specific bout with fear. But I haven't told you all of my fears. In fact, I've kept one of my fears quiet, but I feel like I need to talk about it because it's likely a fear you struggle with as well, and I want to shift the focus to you. I hope that sharing my story has provided inspiration—it's part of my life's purpose—but I want to give you practical suggestions you can take away as well. I want to help you experience the same kind of victory over fear that I have.

That's why I want to start by talking about one of the greatest fears of our current age: uncertainty. The fear of the unknown and what we can't control. It would be natural for me to talk more about my wire walking to make this point, but I want to make this as concrete as possible for you. You will likely never walk a literal wire, but you almost certainly know something about the other wire I constantly walk—financial pressure.

I find my value in God, not in man. But I make my living by doing things that amaze and astound people. I've done some incredible stunts in my life, but with each success, there's a ratcheting pressure because I have to ask myself, *What do I do next that will make people notice me?* If I do the same things I've always done, people will stop paying attention. And if I do the same things others have done, that's of no value because there's no amazement for the audience. That means I have to look for the next big thing, the next amazing stunt, because that's how I pay my bills.

It's what my great-grandfather Karl Wallenda called "a fear of feathers." As an entertainer, you never know when your next paycheck may come in, and my great-grandfather always summed up that tension this way: "One day you eat the chicken, and the next day you eat the feathers."

I remember when my dad lost his trade job. I was a kid, and it was a scary time for our family. We weren't sure where the next meal was going to come from—and I mean that literally. There were some days when, if a member of the church didn't bring something over, we didn't have food. I remember feeling scared during those times and feeling equally scared when we would go to the food bank.

Everyone probably has some memory like that, of a time when things seemed out of control.

Uncertain.

Unknown.

Have you ever felt that? Have you ever carried within you a fear about what the future holds? I think it's common within the heart because we're human—we're limited to what we can see and touch and experience. We can't see out beyond ourselves, which makes us nervous, which leads to fear, which leads to what the writer Henry David Thoreau called "lives of quiet desperation." We end up not living our days to the fullest because we're afraid of something we can't place.

I've dealt with this fear all of my life. Long before the accident in Sarasota, before the Big Apple Circus, before any of the other walks I've done, I've dealt with this fear of uncertainty and learned to channel it, to let it drive me to do great things with my life. It's a real concern for me to continue providing for my family at the level I've been able to. I've done well in my career. I've had some tremendous opportunities that have allowed me to sustain my family and set us up for success down the road. I believe that's what I'm supposed to do as a husband and a father; I'm supposed to do what the Bible calls us to do: leave an inheritance for our children and grandchildren (Prov. 13:22). And that's way more important to me than anybody saying, "Wow, Nik walked over Niagara Falls!"

But in order to make money, I have to continue to do stuff to remain relevant; otherwise the networks and the media will contract with someone else. I keep pushing myself past my limits because of that fear of feathers—I continue to innovate and reinvent myself because that's what it takes to provide for my family.

LESSONS LEARNED FROM FAILURE

Maybe you feel this way too—maybe you feel the weight of uncertainty, that fear of the unknown, but instead of using it to drive you to greater things, you've allowed it to drive you down in a life of quiet desperation. I've seen what that looks like; I've felt that kind of defeat before. And because I have, I know it's not where you want to be. You have a burning desire for things to change, to be different. You want to move beyond the uncertainty and live a better life, but the fear of feathers has got you down.

Just as I had to overcome my fear of falling after the accident in Sarasota, I've learned how to channel this fear of feathers into a strong and healthy mindset that allows me to be successful in life. I want to share some of my observations with you and encourage you to defeat uncertainty. There are three key principles to learn if you want to channel the fear of the unknown into energy for your life.

1. Fight Every Day for What You Want

While I've been writing this book, we've been going through the run-up to a presidential election. A lot of the people running for president have made it their platform to make a lot of things free—health care, college, even a basic income! These campaign promises have resonated especially with younger people, but they've also found a following among people of the working class, those who find them-selves living paycheck to paycheck and are vulnerable any time the economy takes a turn. These promises of free stuff resonate because people crave that security—they want certainty for their lives instead of the uncertainty they've been living with.

But here's the thing: that same uncertainty can propel you to great success. It doesn't have to hold you back. It doesn't have to consign you to a life of fear. If you're sick and tired of life being uncertain, then you can fight like heck to change it. The development of the gig economy showed that if you are willing to hustle and leverage your skills and your time, you can find ways to increase your income. But you have to be willing to do the work. The law of gig economy is if you're not moving, you're not making. You have to fight for what you want.

I'm not just talking about fighting by taking on more and more work. I'm talking about fighting in other ways too. You have to fight against the consumer mentality that says you can spend more than you earn. You have to fight against the advertisers who want you to believe you have to have the latest phone or the fastest car or even the newest shampoo if you want to be successful. There are plenty of forces fighting against you, forces that our culture has declared normal and healthy. The truth is, they're not. They work against your dreams even as they promise to help you achieve them.

I understand this fight because I live it every day. I don't make my income like many people do, working nine to five in an office with a consistent paycheck that hits on the fifteenth and thirtieth of each month. My family has to live differently in order to make what I earn work for us. As a result, we live within our means. By the grace of God, I have literally no debt whatsoever on anything. I pay cash for everything I own. I wake up every day and ask myself, *What's next?* because I understand that if I don't, the gravity of uncertainty will pull me down and seek to keep me that way.

You have to fight a similar fight, even if your circumstances aren't the same as mine. Maybe you do have a job with a steady paycheck, but it's not the job you really want, and you feel like it's killing you inside to just maintain the daily grind. You'd love to change jobs, love to try something new, but the fear of uncertainty keeps you chained to your desk. Your fight is to remember that your life is measured by more than just a paycheck. Yes, earning a living is necessary—we'll talk about the importance of work in the next principle—but being alive to your purpose in life is just as necessary. And no one is going to fight for that on your behalf; you must fight for it yourself, and you must fight for it every day.

Fighting requires sacrifice. It requires doing things differently. It's a mental muscle we develop by giving up things that are comfortable for things that are better. If we don't fight for what we want, we will watch it slip through our fingers like sand. The muscle will slowly deteriorate until there's no fight left in us. So resist that temptation! Find a way, every day, to fight for what you want in some way. Try something new. Say no to something that doesn't matter. Set your priorities and stick to them, even when uncertainty tells you it's too dangerous. It's a high-wire act all its own, and it's one you can walk if you'll try.

2. Work for What You Desire

Once you've made the decision to fight for what you want, you have to put in the work to get what you desire. I don't know about your dreams, but mine didn't come with instructions. There was no simple set of steps for me to take to get to where I wanted to go. I had to figure things out on my own and put in a lot of work. It hasn't always been pleasant, and there were times when I would have preferred things to be easier. But the pathway to our dreams requires effort on our part.

I have mentioned briefly the challenges that came with my desire to walk over Niagara Falls, but the story of what it took fits perfectly here. When the idea came up, politicians on both sides of the border said, essentially, "You'll get permission over my dead body." The laws prohibiting what I was hoping to do had stood on the books for nearly a century. But I went to work on changing the laws—at least for my event—and after working the issue all the way through the legislature in New York, I had to make my way over to Canada to get a waiver there too. The media, the elected officials, and the nonelected ones all stood in the way—until they didn't. When I tell you that getting permission was harder than walking the wire, believe me! But I was willing to do the work, and it became one of the most meaningful walks of my career.

That's true for any dream. I've shared how I've spent my life working to get better at what I do professionally. I spend dozens of hours a week up on a wire, practicing for whatever opportunity is next. I practice in rain, wind, heat, cold—whatever it takes to prepare my mind and my body for what I *might* experience during my next performance. I work hard at my craft, and it's paid off for me over the years.

But wire walking isn't all I do. I work just as hard in

other areas of my life, and truthfully, I work harder because those are newer areas. I have to work at being a business owner. I'm responsible for a lot of people, so being smart in my business decisions is essential. That means I've had to learn payroll, taxes, employment law, budgeting, and other essentials. Sure, I have people to help me, but because the business is my responsibility and the gateway to what I want out of life, I still have to put in work in order to get better.

The same goes for my television specials. I have to work hard at being a producer, since I'm intricately involved in every aspect of each broadcast. I've had to learn TV lingo, navigate contracts, work with camera angles, and think about the safety concerns of my network partners. I've done five specials now, so I know more than I used to, but it still requires me to work hard to stay on top of that part of my life.

I also have to work hard at being a good husband and father. I want to be the best husband I can be, and that means I must constantly work on some of the aspects of myself that cause tension with Erendira. I can be overwhelmingly obsessive about things, and maybe nowhere is that more true than with cleaning. I don't just mop the floors; I remove every single piece of furniture, go over the floors with a brush, and *then* mop it up. That's just the way I do it. That's my thing. When I clean the kitchen, I wipe down every cabinet, clean every inch of counter space, make sure everything is neater than it was. And my wife hates it because it's so over the top to her. To me, it's being a good person, it's living out my faith and representing God by doing everything I can to the very best of my ability. It's just who I am—I'm the kind of guy who keeps his grass cut, his trees trimmed, and his house clean. But I have to balance that with Erendira's wants and needs. I have to work at making sure I'm not just living for myself—no matter how noble I believe my intentions to be—but that I'm living to support and care for her in the ways she needs. The same goes for our kids; I can't be obsessed professional dad all the time, thinking about work or the next project. I have to make time for them and be the person they need me to be, and that takes work on my part.

Nothing worthwhile comes without a price. We have to work for the things we truly desire, and we must do that work daily. When you commit to work for the things you really want, you begin to simultaneously quiet the voice of uncertainty and stir it to scream louder. Because the minute you start working toward your dreams, uncertainty is going to bring up one final trick to keep you stuck. It's going to start screaming at you that you are going to fail, and failure is the one thing your dreams can't afford. It's a lie, of course, because failure is inevitable on your road to success—which is the final principle I want to share with you.

3. Accept That Failure Is Inevitable

Let me start with this: you can't succeed if you never fail. Failure is what results from trying something you've never done or haven't gotten good at. Anyone, no matter how naturally talented or skilled they may be, has to fail in order to succeed. Look no further than a baby learning to walk—toddlers will take several steps and then fall, but inevitably they will get back up and try again until they finally learn to walk. No toddler with the ability to learn to walk has ever given up and settled for crawling as a primary means of getting around. I mean, have you ever seen an adult crawling as a general practice? Of course not! Even as little ones, we understand that failure isn't failure unless you don't get back up.

But that's the problem—so many people don't get back up. We've been taught for a long time that failure is not an option. So when you're thinking about trying something new, or when you're actually trying something new, you suddenly feel a burden to be perfect. After all, if failure isn't an option, that means the only option is success, which means you have to do everything right in order to achieve your goal. And if you fail—or maybe I should say *when* you fail—it's not celebrated as a part of your education but instead is held up as a personal deficiency in your character.

I believe that failure is necessary to achieve greatness. I don't know of any truly successful or memorable people who didn't have a string of failures to their credit. What makes them different isn't that they avoided failure but that they learned from it. Failure can often be our best training tool as long as we react properly. And what is that proper response?

First, we have to *embrace that we failed*. We can't make excuses for it; we can't try to rationalize it away. We have to own the fact that what we were trying to do didn't get done. No one ever succeeded by clinging to excuses, and no one ever moved past a failure by pretending it didn't exist.

That's why the second part of our response to failure is to *examine the failure*. We have to look for the things we did that led to the failure and learn lessons from it. Did you not plan properly? Did you not execute your plan? Did you partner with someone who couldn't deliver as promised, or were you unclear about what you wanted from that partner? Go back over each aspect of the failure and look for the places where you can learn to be better next time.

And the third part of our response to failure is to *make sure there is a next time*! Remember, failure isn't failure unless you choose not to get back up. You must decide that you will try again and do things differently now that you're armed with new information. Maybe you've learned what to avoid; maybe you've learned something new you need to try. It does you no good unless you pick yourself up, dust yourself off, and try for success one more time.

THE CERTAINTY OF UNCERTAINTY

To close this chapter, I want to share a story with you from my family's life. It didn't happen on a wire, but rather with one of my children, and it's one of the clearest examples of confronting the fear of uncertainty that I know of.

Several years ago, I did a regional commercial in Detroit, Michigan, for McDonald's. They were launching a new brand of coffee, and to help promote it, Lijana and I walked together between a couple of cranes. While we were there, the promoters invited us to visit the local children's hospital and then the Ronald McDonald House, which offers lodging and other support services to parents whose children are hospitalized with illness.[1] When I visited with Erendira and saw all the gold leaves on the wall representing the children who had passed while their parents were staying there, I was overcome with emotion. Right away I was like, "Man, when I get to that point where I can help, I want to do something for these families and for these kids."

So fast-forward a bit, to just after my walk over Niagara Falls, which was my first big TV opportunity. My assistant, Joseph, got an email from a gentleman whose son was six at the time. The boy's name was Coulter, and he had just been diagnosed with brain cancer. The doctors expected him to live about six months, and his father wrote to tell me how much Coulter really wanted to watch me walk. His dad struggled with the idea of letting Coulter watch me because what I do is so dangerous, but he ultimately decided to let him. In his email, he wrote about how I was so encouraging to his son that he had to write me about it. The family lived in Corpus Christi, Texas, so I determined to get on a plane and go meet this boy.

My wife and I flew there and met Coulter, spending time with him at the hospital and getting to know his family and learning more about his diagnosis. At the time, I was preparing for the longest walk of my career, a 1,576-foot walk above the Milwaukee Mile Speedway at the Wisconsin State Fair.[2] Three years later, in 2015, Coulter and his family came up to Wisconsin for the walk. I wore a shirt that said, "Go Coulter Go!" on the front and "Never give up!" on the back. Coulter wore a shirt that said, "Go Nic Go!" He walked underneath me on an open path while I walked the wire above. After the walk, I brought him up with me as I spoke to a crowd of about twenty thousand people. Coulter joined me in signing autographs, and his parents watched in amazement. They told me later that Coulter was basically lifeless until he got there, but once he arrived, he was running around with my kids and playing in the parking lot. The change in Coulter really affected his parents.

Fast-forward again: I was getting ready to speak at a church in Charlotte, North Carolina. Erendira and I had kept up with Coulter and stayed in touch as his medical journey continued to twist and turn, but on this day, we were more focused on my trip. Erendira was getting ready to take me to the Sarasota airport, and my son was sitting at the kitchen counter with a cold. He was taking his cough medicine and an antibiotic when he suddenly fell over, passed out, and stopped breathing. I immediately laid him down and started giving him CPR. My wife called 911. Thank God, my son started breathing before the ambulance got there—it was maybe sixty seconds at most that he wasn't breathing, but for me it felt like two years.

After the ambulance arrived, we headed to the hospital. The doctors said, "Look, we're going to run every test we can—an MRI, a CT scan, everything you can imagine, because we know you need to get on your trip. We're going to clear him and figure out what this was." They ran a bunch of tests within thirty minutes and said, "He's clear. We believe it was a mix between the antibiotics and the cough medicine that he took, so you can go get on the plane. He's fine."

I got in the car, hurried to the airport, and boarded the plane. Not long after the doors closed and the plane was getting ready for takeoff, my phone rang. It was Erendira. I answered quietly (those flight attendants still don't like it when your phone goes off!), and she said, "We're in the back of an ambulance on our way to All Children's Hospital."

"What do you mean? The doctor said everything was fine."

"No," Erendira said. "They found a lump in his chest. And they want us at All Children's immediately."

This is when the fear of the unknown struck. I mean, I was helpless, stuck in an airplane, about to be miles away from my family—not that I could have done anything even if I had been sitting there in the ambulance. My mind raced the entire flight, and as soon as I landed in Charlotte, I called Erendira and said, "I'm going to rent a car. It's a thirteen-hour drive, but I have got to get back home."

She said, "Nope, you're called to do God's work, and you need to stay there. This is just a test."

I began to cry. My son was sick, I was hundreds of miles away, and my wife was encouraging me to stick it out, referring to what we were up against as a "test." Talk about faith! I can tell you honestly that it was the hardest thing I've ever done. That decision to stay and speak took every ounce of faith and courage I had. My appearance at the church was interview-style, which is the way I usually do presentations, and it was extremely emotional. I think everybody in the congregation was crying. Before it was over, my tears weren't about my son; they were just my emotions coming out. I was a wreck. Fear and uncertainty were dragging me down. But I fought through it, did the work I promised to do, and realized that being separated from my family in a moment of crisis was a new lesson in my journey.

I flew to Tampa as soon as I could after the event, and

then I went straight to All Children's in St. Petersburg. Once I got there, the doctor said, "We want to meet with you later on this evening." Nothing worse than being told to hold on while your child is in a hospital bed. When the staff finally ushered us back to a private room, the doctor said, "We think that this is cancerous. We need to do a lot more research, and we have reason to be very concerned."

I can't describe what Erendira and I felt in that moment. We just had these thoughts of, *It's out of our control.* And, as you've probably gathered, I like to be in control of *everything.* We hunkered down at the hospital, and after a week of tests and scans, doctors found that our son was suffering a severe case of walking pneumonia that looked like a mass on X-rays and scans. I praised God for the news, but I can tell you the panic that we went through over the course of those ten days drew me closer to other parents. It made me think more often of Coulter's parents, or those parents at the Ronald McDonald House who find out that, for their kids, it *is* cancer. And for some of those parents, it means saying goodbye.

I know there is a reason for everything that happens, and it's up to us whether we want to find the opportunity within that uncertainty and turn it into something good. I believe that what happened with my son—just like the accident in Sarasota—happened for a bigger purpose. That's why I'm writing this book. In everything, even fear and uncertainty, we can find that reason—if we have courage enough to face that fear and learn to overcome it.

CHAPTER 9

FACE YOUR FEAR

LET'S START WITH THIS: FEAR IS A NATURAL HUMAN response.

I grew up in a family that handled fear in a certain way, but we never pretended it wasn't human to feel fear—we just recognized that it wasn't always helpful. Every human being is equipped with the ability to experience fear, and often that fear is what we need to change our circumstances for the better. As I said in the previous chapter, fear happens for a reason—and what it produces is all about how we respond to it. That's not only true mentally, emotionally, and spiritually, but it's true physically as well.

I've mentioned the fight-or-flight response that everyone experiences when presented with uncertainty and danger. We're wired to either fight against the threat we're facing or run away from it in the hopes of surviving another day. Some people are geared more toward fight responses, while others are geared more toward flight responses, but there are times when people must choose against their wiring—times when fighters must flee and flighters must fight. How you respond depends on what you need to do to survive.

The more I write about my journey and dig into the lessons I've learned, the more I've come to realize that a lot of what my family was teaching against wasn't the emotion of fear; it was the expression of panic. When fear goes unchecked, it evolves into panic, and panic is dangerous. As I write this, we're in the middle of the COVID-19 pandemic, something unlike anything any of us have ever experienced. Who had ever heard of *social distancing* or *shelter in place* before? But we've had to make some changes, no matter how irrational they felt at first. Early on we saw otherwise intelligent and reasoned people gripped by fear, even to the point of panic. Grocery stores were emptied of toilet paper, bottled water, and other basic necessities as fear of the unknown took hold of people. Panic is often useless because it prevents you from attacking the fear in a helpful way—instead of fighting or flighting, you end up frozen in the emotion, stuck in a problem you don't want to have.

This is what my parents wanted Lijana and me to avoid on the wire. They didn't want us frozen in panic, trapped in a state where our actions weren't *actions* but rather *reactions* we couldn't control. They wanted us to be in control of our fear and, by extension, immune to panic; they wanted us to have the ability to walk out on that wire with clear heads and steady feet. I understand that not everyone can operate that way, and even if you can, it's not always healthy to do so. There's danger in believing you're beyond fear. But when you place fear in the proper perspective, you can possess a definite peace of mind.

There's a great story from the Bible that illustrates this. In the twelfth chapter of Acts, one of Jesus' followers named Peter was thrown in prison by the Roman-appointed ruler of Israel, King Herod. Peter was going around Jerusalem talking about Jesus and sharing about his death, burial, and resurrection, and Herod didn't like it at all. In fact, Herod hated the people who were talking about the church, and he'd previously killed one of Peter's friends, a man named James. The Bible says Herod had James put to death by sword.

So Peter was in danger. A lot of danger. It would make sense that once he was in prison, his mind would race with fear and anxiety over what was going to happen to him. After all, James was dead—and Peter was probably going to be next! Most normal people would be going crazy in that cell, trying to think about what might happen or what they might do to get out of the situation. The stress of the unknown—especially when the unknown seems likely to be execution—would make most people go out of their minds with fear.

But not Peter.

The Bible says that Peter fell asleep in his prison cell. In fact, it was the night before he was supposed to appear before King Herod for his sentencing, and Peter fell asleep between two guards assigned to keep watch over him! What kind of peace does it take to fall asleep on the night before your likely death? Where does that kind of peace come from?

I believe it comes from facing your fear and knowing that you can beat it. Peter knew that death wasn't something for him to fear, because he'd already faced that fear before when he watched his friend and teacher Jesus die. The night before Jesus was crucified on the cross, Peter was in the courtyard where Jesus was being tried. Someone recognized Peter as one of Jesus' followers, and Peter denied it—three times! He let his fear of death cause him to betray his Savior, and it shattered his life. It wasn't until Jesus appeared to Peter after his resurrection that Peter was able to confess his fear and face it. Jesus forgave him and gave him the courage to face his eventual death, which is why Peter was able to fall asleep in that prison. He had faced his fear and moved beyond it.

There's a healthy process for facing your fear and learning how to move past it, and I want to share it with you.

CALL YOUR FEAR BY NAME

Just like Peter, it helps to know what enemy you're facing. I'm not a psychologist or a therapist by any stretch of the imagination, but I know that giving your fear a name is an essential first step to overcoming it. When fear is undefined, it wreaks havoc with your heart and mind, and you cannot make healthy or helpful decisions if that's the case. From an early age, I knew that falling was a fear I had to overcome, and it was easy to name that fear because of our family history. Once I named the fear, it was easy

Nik and Lijana at SeaWorld San Diego; Nik's first public performance.

Terry and Delilah holding Nik and Lijana on the wire at Circus Vargas.

Nik on the wire with help of mom, Delilah, backstage at Circus Vargas.

Nik and Lijana performing as teenagers at Americana Amusement Park.

Nik walking a wire in 2013 across the Grand Canyon at world-record height.

Nik Wallenda, Blake Wallenda, and Khera Smith perform on opening night at Circus Sarasota, two days after the accident.

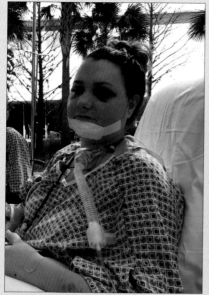

Nik Wallenda

Tom Rhein

Lijana's in the Sarasota Memorial Hospital courtyard, her first time outside less than a week after the fall.

Nik walks over Amalie Arena for It Works!, two days after the accident.

Delilah Wallenda

Nik and Lijana are interviewed on the *TODAY* show upon Lijana's first visit to the Circus Sarasota tent several weeks after the accident.

Nik and Lijana practice the crossover for Times Square at Nathan Benderson Park.

Norm Schimmel

Joseph Mascitto

Practicing at Nathan Benderson Park in front of a crowd for the first time since the accident as she prepares for the Times Square walk.

Nik and Lijana among the skyscrapers around Times Square.

Nik and Lijana near the midpoint of the wire over Times Square.

Nik crosses over Lijana at the midpoint of the wire high above Times Square.

Nik and Lijana over the expanse of Times Square.

Lijana on the wire over Times Square.

Nik, Lijana, and family at the press conference following the Times Square walk.

Nik completes his longest walk at the time (2015) over the Wisconsin State Fair.

Nik and Terry work to attach Erendira's lyra to the safety cable over the Masaya volcano.

Erendira tests her lyra before moving out over the volcano.

Nik watches and communicates with Erendira as she performs over the volcano.

Nik in protective gear during the walk over Masaya.

Tim Boyles

Nik around the midpoint of the cable over the lava lake of the Masaya volcano.

for me to compartmentalize it and press forward with my performances.

Or there's the fear of uncertainty, the fear of the unknown, like we talked about in chapter 8. I find this to be one of the most common fears I come across, and yet it's often challenging for people to give this fear a name. As I've mentioned, I'm a control freak; I don't like the feeling of being out of control, and it's very easy for me to fight against that feeling instead of owning up to it. But the longer I pretend like everything's fine, or the longer I simply try to get control over something that's beyond me, the longer it takes me to recover. It's better for me and for the people I love if I admit that I'm afraid of the uncertainty. Once I name the fear, I know how to face it, and so does everyone around me.

Your fear might not be as sneaky as the fear of uncertainty or as obvious as a fear of falling, but it has a name regardless. Maybe it's a fear of failure. Maybe it's a fear of success. Maybe it's a fear of intimacy in relationships, or a fear of sickness or death. Or maybe you've never allowed yourself to sit down and think about it long enough to give your fear a name. Wherever you find yourself, you need to invest the time in figuring out what your specific fear is, because without a name, it will be difficult to move forward.

Fear works in generalities; it torments you with "What if . . . ?" and "What about . . . ?" because that's its nature. It preys on what you can't control. But it loses its power when it's connected to a thought or idea. Give your fear a name, and you'll be able to find a solution.

TALK ABOUT YOUR FEAR OUT LOUD

Once you've given your fear a name, talk about it out loud. This sounds a little strange, but I'm not suggesting a conversation with your fear (though you're welcome to give that a try). I'm suggesting you find someone who will give you an empathetic ear and allow you to share what's on your mind. The more you can talk about your fear, the more you can rob the fear of its emotional power.

This works different ways for different people. We live in an age where it's most common to talk about your fear with a therapist or counselor. There are plenty of qualified professionals to choose from for in-person visits, as well as the option to talk to someone online. As I mentioned, therapy was not for me, but that doesn't mean it's not for you. I ended up speaking to my wife, my family, and my pastor. I turned to voices I knew I could trust and people who knew me. It's what worked best for me. Maybe you're not close to your family like I am, so that avenue isn't one you can safely go down. But there are other options, and there's a good chance that talking to someone, be it a psychologist, a friend, a pastor, or a counselor, is the right thing for you.

Regardless of whether you talk to a counselor, there's someone I definitely can recommend talking to, and that's God. As I've mentioned throughout the book, my faith is everything to me, and my ability to talk to God about the things I'm facing and trying to overcome is an essential part of my growth. The Bible encourages us to pray about our anxieties, something that I believe too few people take seriously.

Here are some scriptures to consider:

- First Peter 5:7 says, "Cast all your anxiety on him [Jesus] because he cares for you." *Anxiety* is another word for fear that's out of control—an abnormal and overwhelming sense of apprehension and terror. We experience it when we don't know what the future holds, when our fears cause us to question whether things will work out for us. Jesus knows what your future holds because he knows what your future is. You can cast your fears on him because he can set them to rest with his knowledge and power.

- Matthew 11:28–30 says, "Come to me, all you who are weary and burdened, and I will give you rest. Take my yoke upon you and learn from me, for I am gentle and humble in heart, and you will find rest for your souls. For my yoke is easy and my burden is light." This is a personal invitation from Jesus himself to bring your fears to him, because fears are a burden to anyone who carries them. You weren't made to struggle alone through this world; he cares about what you're feeling, he cares about the fears that are choking you, and he wants to help you overcome them. In fact, he helps you overcome them by carrying them for you—he partners with you as the stronger one and lightens the load on your shoulders.

- Philippians 4:6–7 says, "Do not be anxious about anything, but in every situation, by prayer and petition, with thanksgiving, present your requests to God. And the peace of God, which transcends all understanding, will guard your hearts and your minds in Christ Jesus." These verses cut to the heart of why talking to God about our fears is such a helpful thing to do—it tells us that when we bring our fears and anxieties to God in prayer, his peace guards our hearts and minds. We give God our worries, and he gives us a peace that we can't fully understand. The situation that sparked the fear may not be resolved, but the fear is conquered because God's peace covers us.

If you find it hard to pray about your fear, or if you don't feel comfortable seeking counsel, another way to talk about it is to write in a journal or notebook. You could also try recording yourself talking through the thoughts that are running through your head without trying to make sense of them. Categorizing what's scaring you by writing out in detail the things you're afraid of, or recording them on your phone, helps your mind think through the problem with clarity rather than emotion.

TAKE CONTROL OF YOUR THOUGHTS

Fears emanate from your mind, which means that your mind can help you overcome them if you give it a chance. If you want to move beyond your fear, you have to learn to discipline your mind. Your mind can be your biggest enemy or your biggest asset—it's truly up to you. If you want your mind to be your friend, you'll have to take control of the way you think.

Many people aren't intentional with their thinking; they allow whatever thoughts bubble up into their minds to have priority, as if they have no control over what they think about. I fully believe that your mind is something you must protect and take charge of; in the Bible, the apostle Paul wrote in his letter to the Philippian church that we must take control over what we think.

Paul put it this way: "Finally, brothers and sisters, whatever is true, whatever is noble, whatever is right, whatever is pure, whatever is lovely, whatever is admirable—if anything is excellent or praiseworthy—think about such things" (Phil. 4:8).

Notice what Paul said we should think about: things that are true, noble, right, pure, lovely, and admirable—it's essentially the original call to the power of positive thinking! The content we think about has the power to transform our minds, something that Paul wrote about in his letter to the Romans when he said, "Be transformed by the renewing of your mind" (Rom. 12:2). If you're tired of thinking negative, self-defeating thoughts that are darkened by fear, then you have to turn your thoughts to good, noble, and right things in order to renew your mind. It's a challenge, because for some people, the power of positive thinking is really just the power of denying negative thoughts. But denial doesn't help you grow; denial doesn't renew your mind. Only turning your thoughts to things that are good and healthy can do that.

Learning to renew your mind this way is crucial because, in my experience, there are plenty of people who will go out of their way to challenge your thinking and make you doubt. This has happened to me before some of my walks. People always focus on the potential negative outcomes, the possibilities of my failing and falling. I understand why they ask—they simply cannot imagine doing what I do because they cannot imagine overcoming what I've overcome. Their minds go only to the dark and negative places, and that's where they expect me to go when they ask questions. But negativity is a vacuum—it will suck you in and hold you there. It's a trap that will disengage you from your visions and goals. That's why I always encourage people to remove anyone and anything negative from their lives. You can't live in the negative realm and overcome your fears, which means you can't be around people who live there. Negative people will always want you to be negative.

But the truth is, you can't always remove *everyone* who adds some negativity to your life. Sometimes it is just a piece of the job. A key requirement of all these big walks I've done over the last several years has been doing pre-event media sessions. And while I have complete respect for what the media has to do, I'd be lying if I didn't tell you that many of these sessions and the questions that come with them have an impact on my mindset.

Can you imagine being asked things like "Do you have a death wish?" "Do you want to die on live TV?" "What if the winds are so strong that there is no way you'll make it?" just hours before getting ready to walk out over Times Square?

I have *actually* been asked each of those questions! And yes, they do mess with my mind. That's where developing this specific discipline is an absolute necessity.

Disciplining your mind will require sacrifices, but it will

give you freedom. Start by writing down your thoughts so you can examine them. Take an hour and write down everything that comes into your head, without filtering it. Then, after the hour is up, take a look at what you've written down. Is it mostly positive or mostly negative? Full of doubt or full of faith? Look at the pattern because you'll need to either break it or encourage it, depending on whether it's building you up toward what's good.

When you discipline your thoughts and where you allow them to go, you begin to move in the direction of your dreams. This discipline is crucial because it is the foundation for your future, and when you have a firm foundation, even if you fall, you get back up that much quicker. Build a firm foundation by surrounding yourself with positive people and positive things. Fill your mind with positive music and messages, positive words and images. Avoid putting destructive or hurtful junk into your brain, because what you put in you'll inevitably get out.

TAKE CONTROL OF YOUR EMOTIONS

Controlling your emotions comes after thinking because how you think in large part determines how you feel. If your brain is constantly muddled with negative thoughts, it's a sure bet your emotions are going to follow suit. Once you learn to think positively and take control over what goes into and comes out of your brain, you'll find that your emotions will begin to mirror that change. Proverbs 4:23–26 makes this connection clear:

Above all else, guard your heart,
for everything you do flows from it.
Keep your mouth free of perversity;
keep corrupt talk far from your lips.
Let your eyes look straight ahead;
fix your gaze directly before you.
Give careful thought to the paths for your feet
and be steadfast in all your ways.

Notice how the writer said to "guard your heart"? In ancient times, the heart was considered the source of thoughts and emotions, so the writer was cautioning readers to be careful about what goes into their hearts, because what goes in will inevitably come out. Just as we have to be careful with the types of thoughts we think, we need to be careful with our emotions. While they are an essential part of the way we're made, they aren't always reliable; we can be swayed by emotion to say and do things we might otherwise regret, and since fear is such a powerful emotion, we need to be especially careful about the influence we give it in our hearts.

If this feels like too much for you, or if you're having trouble wrapping your mind around the concept, that's okay. I haven't walked in your shoes, so I can only tell you what has worked for me, what I've learned through the challenges I've faced. I have found that my emotions are much easier to guide and control when my thinking is healthy and upbeat.

Now, that's not to say I don't have my bad days. Everyone does! But I also know that practice makes perfect, and I strive for perfection. I want my emotional response to the things that happen to me to be in line with my thinking, and I want all of my mind and heart to be in line with my visions and dreams. That's the secret to any successful individual—everyone who achieves something in life believes that they have the ability to do it, and that belief is fueled by the alignment of their thoughts and emotions.

I've found that the fastest way to healthy control over my emotions comes through gratitude and praise. I think focusing on the things that are good and healthy in my life allows me to feel good and healthy about my life. I give thanks for my wife and children. I give thanks for my mom and dad. I give thanks for my sister. I give thanks for the incredible people who have come alongside to support me as I build my dreams. I give thanks for my ability to walk the wire. I give thanks for my hunger for significance and success. I could go on and on, but the point is that as I turn my mind and heart toward the things that are good in my life, I am able to see other good things around me. We find our opportunities where we turn our gaze, and if we're looking at and for good things, we'll find good opportunities.

I want to help you live your best story. I don't know what visions or dreams you have for your life—assuming that you have them at all—but I know that if you haven't lived them out, there's a strong chance it's because you haven't dealt with your fear. We live in a culture that praises dreamers and their dreams but then goes out of its way to tear them down; it's a profitable self-defeating culture. Anxiety is one of the most common forms of mental illness in America, with forty million people affected.[1] Of those forty million, fewer than 37 percent seek help to deal with it, which means the majority simply live with their anxiety.[2] People are crippled by this condition, and what is sad is that they don't have to be.

You don't have to be.

You can overcome your fears. You can find strength to move forward with your life. You can live down and out with the negative thoughts and emotions that tell you life will never go your way. Or you can choose to live differently. It doesn't matter how many times you've fallen, how many times you believe you've failed; there is hope for you and the life you want to live.

CHAPTER 10

FIND YOUR FOOTING

IT JUST MAKES SENSE FOR A GUY WHO WALKS ON wires for a living to write a chapter about finding your footing, doesn't it?

Of course, I'm not talking about where you place your actual feet; this is more about finding your emotional and mental balance as you seek to move past your fears. I love a saying commonly attributed to Sir Winston Churchill: "Fear is a reaction. Courage is a decision." Courage is the ability to act in the face of fear, to take a single step forward when everything in you wants to take a step backward. If we are going to grow beyond fear, we've got to find our footing.

We've got to develop the twin virtues of courage and faith in order to move toward our dreams, and then we've got to settle in ourselves the core beliefs that we hold about life. We have to decide what we believe about the world and how we choose to see it. The stronger and better our foundation, the more we can achieve.

In some ways, it's like rigging a high wire.

One of the biggest contributors to my success, one of the main reasons why I've been able to do these amazing walks, is all of the work that goes on behind the scenes. Yes, my ability to walk the wire is what draws the crowds, but I wouldn't be able to walk in the first place if I didn't have a secure wire. I can convince TV execs and local authorities to let me do things they generally wouldn't allow, but the only way I'm able to do that is by giving them confidence in me and my knowledge that I know what I'm doing.

When I first started out, people needed a lot of convincing, and showing them the care and technical skill in how my team and I rig my wires was a big piece of evidence I could point to. Now that my career has progressed, it's a lot easier because the word is out. They've seen what I've done; they've seen that it's real. And it's all because of our engineering and my incredible uncle, Mike Troffer. Uncle Mike is an engineer himself, and he designs my equipment with my specific needs in mind.

In the circus world, a very small percentage of equipment is designed and stamped by a professional engineer. But thanks to my dad, my uncle, and our family's history of engineering minds, everything we do with my gear uses technology to our advantage. It provides me with stronger, safer wires, and we continue to advance our knowledge with every new event. The advancements in engineering have certainly helped my career, and when we combine those advancements with my experience and the people that are on my team, we get the ability to tackle great challenges quickly. So when we come in and present something, it is *solid.* We're not going to do anything that local officials or my production partners will have to worry about.

Usually when I'm pitching a walk, I give a presentation to the officials of the city or country where I'm hoping to walk. I usually include the opportunity for officials to sit around a conference table with my team and ask questions. One of my team or I will look around the room and ask, "What roadblocks do you see?" We want to know why the department of buildings might consider saying no, why the department of engineering might say no, why the fire marshal might say no, and so on down the line. It's our job to get the objections out in the open so we can carefully address them. Then, once we hear their concerns, we give them a solution for each objection. After a while, we learned what the most common objections were, so we just built them into our presentation. It makes us very effective and instills even greater confidence. It is what any good sales professional would do.

I went to a meeting once with about sixty City of Chicago government officials. The room was full of people—representatives from the department of transportation, the fire marshal, some of the aldermen, even the mayor's assistant. You name it, they were there. I was partnering at the time with the Discovery Channel, and I was hoping to convince city officials to allow me to walk between skyscrapers downtown . . . blindfolded!

After we exchanged pleasantries, some of my partners from the Discovery Channel spoke, telling those gathered how we wanted to do a live television special. During my presentation, I focused on the fine details of how the wire rigging works, why it works, why it would be successful, and how it would not affect the city in a negative way. When I was done, we gave everyone a chance to ask questions.

"Alderman, do you have questions?"

"Nope. Everything's good."

"Okay, how about you, Fire Marshal. Do you have a question?"

"Nope."

"Police Chief?"

"No."

One by one we went around the room. No one had questions. No one had any concerns whatsoever.

After my team and I left the meeting and headed to lunch with some of Discovery Channel's vice presidents, someone said, "Something's wrong. Something's seriously wrong. Everyone around that table said, 'Okay', or 'Nope, nothing wrong.' That's not normal."

I wasn't surprised by the lack of questions or concerns because I know that the way we rig our wires and the preparation work we do is solid. Secure. Strong. When I walk, there may be dozens of different variables for me to consider, but I am able to step onto each and every wire with confidence because I know how it's built and how it's anchored. I can find my footing because my wire is secure.

That's what core values do for your life—they give you sure footing. They allow you to walk with confidence and try new and greater things. Core values can be anything that you sincerely hold true—things like integrity, fairness, honesty. Some people have a core value of fun, while others hold faith and family as the values dearest to them. You can have as many core values as you'd like, but what truly makes each one a core value is that it influences *all* of your decisions on a daily basis. You're intentional about living them out in everything you do. Maybe you get your core values from your religious faith, or maybe you get them from your community or family upbringing, or maybe your core values are developed over time as you grow and mature. However you come to them, they are an essential part of how you learn to navigate life.

I'm going to share with you some of my core values, not because they need to be yours, but so you can understand how they impact my life. Hopefully, they will inspire you to dig in and identify your own.

PERSEVERANCE

I fully believe that if you want to succeed in life, you have to learn to persevere. Developing the ability to stay with things, especially hard things, is essential for growth and success. I think back to my childhood and learning how to walk on the wire. The walking part came naturally, but there were so many other aspects that took me time to learn and perfect. There's balance, there's how to adjust, there's the mental stamina required to deal with things that aren't going your way.

And then there's learning how to fall. It sounds like it should be simple—after all, gravity does most of the work—but there's a right way that takes time to master. The key is falling *to* the wire, not *off* the wire. If you fall *to* the wire, you can grab hold and effectively stop the fall before it begins. If you fall off, that means falling away from the wire, which means losing the chance to catch it. I think back to Sarasota; when the pyramid collapsed, I went *to* the wire and was able to hang on. Lijana fell *off* the wire, and so her fall was much worse. The dynamic of the eight-person pyramid and her spot in that pyramid also played a big role in how she fell, and I'm in no way suggesting her training wasn't good, because we were both taught to fall to the wire, but sometimes it doesn't always work out.

Learning to fall is scary—and tedious. It takes the right kind of attitude to intentionally get on a wire and throw yourself toward the ground, over and over again. It's a test of your will, which is what perseverance is—a person's willingness to grind out the tough and challenging circumstances of life. Part of what fuels my perseverance is understanding that my life is lived for a bigger purpose. That confidence allows me to try new things, to stretch myself, and honestly, to fail a lot. It would be so easy to allow each of those failures to discourage me; after all, most people don't try things with the intention of being bad at them. But because I'm set in my purpose, every time I fail I can quickly recover. It's like falling off the wire during practice—I could get discouraged, but instead I get back up because I know why I'm doing it and what it will produce if I stick with it.

It has also helped not only to learn how to fall but to admit it when I do. It's easy to own up to falling when I'm practicing on the wire—that's just par for the course, if not expected when I am constantly training in the absolute worst conditions possible. But it's much harder to own up to falling in other areas. Yet over time I've learned that if I'm trying something new or something that I know will stretch me, it's better to quickly say, "Hey, I failed," if things don't go my way. It does two things—it lets people know that I'm aware that I made a mistake, and it relieves them of the burden of having to tell me! To me, it's just being genuine, and yet I find some people are shocked that I'm vulnerable and open when I'm on TV or write about some of my struggles. Some people sincerely believe that we're better off when we try to hide, but to me there's no reason for that because we're all going through *something*. We're all trying to get through the day or the week. How much better would it be if we knew we weren't alone in our struggles?

The reality is we all slip, we all trip, we all fall, and likewise we all need to get back up. We're all trying to get to the other side of our particular wire—whether that's a bad workweek, a tough medical diagnosis, or a season when our finances just aren't quite enough—and there are going to be moments when we fall. But the key is falling *to* the wire, not *off*. We have to train for the fall and discipline ourselves to persevere through the experience so we can catch the wire and then get back up. If I could sum up the secret to wire walking—to life, really—it's this: *keep going until you get to the other side*. You have to persevere. You have to keep putting one foot in front of the other. That's a lesson you can learn not just from me but from my grandmother. Her life was filled with challenges and setbacks, but they prepared her for being diagnosed with cancer. Persevering through her early struggles made her so strong that something like cancer wasn't a big deal to her. The diagnosis was shocking, but she grabbed the wire and held on for the next four years, all the while trying to get back up. She didn't get as long as she wanted, but at least she grabbed on. She didn't just give up and let go.

FAITH

By now, you fully grasp that I'm a person of faith, and it is one of my core values. I believe that I was made by God for a unique purpose, and it's through a relationship with his Son, Jesus Christ, that I am empowered to live out that purpose. I've talked about different types of fear and how we can move past them, but I do think there's one type of fear that's a respectful fear: our fear of God. Because God is perfect and holy, we have to respect him and the magnitude of who he is and his capabilities, but we also love him and choose to worship and seek him. I believe that one day I will have to give an account for my life, so it's essential for me to live knowing that I can ask for forgiveness and constantly pursue God. I live to bring him glory.

That's what my life is about now, but it was a struggle when I was younger—how could I live to bring glory to his name? It's my calling to lead and direct others to God, but I just couldn't see how he was going to use a tightrope walker to do that. But over the years, God has made it clear how he can use me.

When I was walking across Niagara Falls, there were around thirteen other wire walkers who had tried or were trying to get permission to make the crossing. Some of them were trying at the same time I was, but none of them were making headway. I remember saying to God, "God, I don't understand—you've given me verses like Psalm 37:4, which says, 'Take delight in the LORD, and he will give you the desires of your heart,' and Proverbs 3:5–6, which says, 'Trust in the LORD with all your heart, and lean not on your own understanding; in all your ways acknowledge Him, and He shall direct your paths'" (NKJV).

The key is the part that says "lean not on your own understanding; in all your ways acknowledge Him." As I questioned God, I was leaning on my own understanding. I was saying to him, "I feel like you gave me the desire to walk over Niagara Falls, but how are you going to get glory out of this? How is this good for you?" I didn't know how he would work things out, how laws would literally be changed in my favor to allow me to cross, or how many people would end up watching around the world.

As I walked across the falls, I praised God and talked to God, because that's where I find my peace. And as I did that, ABC, one of the most secular networks in the world, didn't bleep it out. They just let it flow, and after the special aired, I received emails from people saying how much I made a difference to them. I remember one email said, "I haven't gotten out of my wheelchair to use my walker in years, and I took the first five steps after I saw Nik walk in the name of Jesus!"

There are other stories like that, stories that come in whenever I do a big walk, and I'm always amazed at how God uses me to touch the lives of millions of people—and how there is always someone within those millions who feels God speak to them through me. That only happens because I don't bury my faith. I don't hide it—it's who I am, and because I live true to that value, God uses me to bring him glory. It's an awesome feeling.

INTEGRITY

By now you know I am a man of my word. If I tell you I'm going to do something, you can count on me doing it, and doing it to the best of my ability. I believe excellence and integrity go hand in hand, because God calls us to be excellent in all we do. That's why I always want not just to deliver on my word but to *over*deliver. I never want to do less than I've promised, and I always promise to do my best.

As a result, I'm constantly having to stretch myself. Every time I do a stunt that's never been done before, I reset the bar for my best. My standard of excellence gets that much higher, and so I have to continually find new ways of being my best. For example, Michael Jordan doesn't pursue greatness on a basketball court today. He did when he was twenty-five or twenty-six, and he left a mark on basketball that maybe no one will ever touch. (I can hear the LeBron and Kobe fans firing up Twitter right now!) But today he measures his best differently. Today he wants to be the first African American team owner to win an NBA title. He wants to continue to grow his business success and his global brand, which pushes him constantly.

I am firmly convinced that your greatest achievements begin the moment you take the first step out of your comfort zone. That's what I do every time I get on the wire—I push myself and my skills further and further. I know some people think, *Oh, he's just walking on a wire. It's all the same no matter where he does it.* But the reality is, when I walked over Niagara Falls, I was stepping out of my comfort zone. Way out. When I walked over Chicago blindfolded, I was stepping out of my comfort zone. When I walked over the Grand Canyon, I was stepping out of my comfort zone. And when I walked over Times Square, I was stepping out of my comfort zone.

Every time I get on the wire, it's not as though I go, *Gosh, this is easy!* It's not like I'm comfortable when I get on the line. I'm always walking into the unknown. Every single walk I do, I don't know what it's going to be like. I don't know what a TV walk will be like before I do it live on TV because I've never done that walk before the cameras start rolling. There are no practice runs for those events. I prepare for my TV walks—but not at the actual site. There are always so many unknowns.

I do this because that's how I grow. It's how I live authentically, true to the person God created me to be. I can't live with integrity and do things halfway. I bring excellence to everything I do, and that need for excellence keeps me pushing my boundaries to grow.

POSITIVITY

One of my other core values is positivity. As I wrote in the previous chapter, it's up to you to control your mind, which means positivity is a mental discipline. The human mind naturally drifts to the negative; it's as if that's the way we're programmed. I don't know why, but I see this in myself most often when I get in an argument with my wife. Any time we get into a disagreement, one of the first places my mind goes is to all the negatives of twenty-plus years spent together, not to all the positive stuff that absolutely outweighs them.

So I have to fight negativity, especially on the wire. Whenever I get up on a wire, if I'm not careful, my mind automatically goes, *What if?* and what follows is always a negative thought. I never ask myself positive questions: *What if the anchors are stronger than they've ever been? What if the winds are calmer than I've ever experienced?* I get up on the wire, and instead it's always, *What if something goes wrong? What if you're not prepared? What if you didn't train right?*

Negativity is where fear comes from. It starts when our minds play out the worst that could happen. I think a lot of fear is conceptual. Some people are scared to drive because they could get into an accident. Some are scared to go to ball games because there could be a terrorist attack. People are scared of flying because the plane could crash. And yet how many plane crashes happen a year in the United States? Statistically, it's very, very few for the major airlines that most people fly. The fear isn't rooted in reality but in the negative spaces of our minds, because that's the way our minds are trained to go.

That's why positivity is one of my core values. I believe that if I train and then discipline my mind to lean the other way, I can prevent my thoughts from going negative, and I can remove a lot of the fear that would do me harm. And even when my thoughts start to go negative, I can counter them with positivity and with reality. I can look at the statistics that are on my side of planes crashing, look at the facts of the situation, look at all the good times with my wife, rather than focusing on the negatives. I can focus on what's true and good and uplifting. That is the kind of person I want to be.

I'm not saying I've mastered this, but as I've gotten older and matured, I've made it a point to work doubly hard at not getting mad or overly negative in any situation. Do I stumble sometimes? Yes. But I've learned to quickly ask forgiveness and then correct my thinking.

One night when Erendira and I were getting ready for bed, my son said, "Hey, Dad, which phone are you giving me?"

I was caught off guard. "What do you mean?"

"I was wondering which of your phones you were going to give me. I'd like to look at it."

Now, I didn't stand there and have a conversation with him. Instead, I went straight to Erendira. "I'm giving him a phone?"

"Yeah, I told him you would give him your phone. He needs one."

And I said, "What do you *mean*?" But my tone wasn't calm or cool or positive, and it started an argument. Voices raised for a few minutes as we aired frustrations with each other, until she walked away to go take a shower. Meanwhile, I put on worship music to calm myself down. I told myself, *I'm not going to go there. I'm not going to allow myself to blow up over something stupid. Who cares about a phone? In the end, it doesn't matter.* But for a moment there, I was tempted to get mad and go to bed ticked off.

The Bible talks about not letting the sun go down on your anger, which is why I used to irritate my wife after we had an argument. I'd tell her, "I'm not letting you go to sleep until you give me a kiss. Because I don't know if I'm going to wake up in the morning, and you don't know if you're going to wake up in the morning. So we're not going to let that anger stay between us."

When Erendira came out of the bathroom, I asked her forgiveness. And the next day, my son got a used phone.

I've practiced the power of positivity so much that it comes a little more naturally now. It's like falling on the wire; when I get in an argument or disagreement, if I catch myself and turn my thoughts toward the positive, it's easier to get back up.

It's amazing how we can control where we allow our minds to go. If I'm struggling with negative thoughts, I love to put on worship music and tell myself, *I'm not going there. I'm not going to allow myself to go negative for no reason.* So I'll listen to worship music and I'll pray, and I'll ask God not to allow those thoughts to overtake me.

Still, the negative can be redeemed if we just accept that God can use everything. We can use our failures, we can use our mistakes, we can use those situations when we're less than our best. Because the other option is to give up. To say, "That's it. I'm not getting back up." Instead, we can say, "No, I'm not going to be defeated. I'll use this to bring glory to his name, and he will use this." And God is faithful—he will use the negative to create something positive. He's done it in my life, time and time again. If my family's history has taught me anything, it's that God redeems. After all, it was a catastrophic fall that prompted this book.

And he can do so much more if we just stay positive about that truth.

Fear is not final; it's a feeling, and feelings can be changed. In fact, you can change your feelings right now with one simple act: a smile. According to several different studies, a smile can change the chemistry in your brain by releasing chemicals that make you happy.[1]

You don't have to live with fear. You can rise above it, and it begins by facing it and taking steps to discipline yourself against it. Once you've done that, you'll find that fear gives way to faith, and that's what it takes to find your footing as you move forward into your new life. That's why we're going to talk about your future in the next chapter.

CHAPTER 11

FOCUS ON YOUR FUTURE

ONCE YOU'VE FACED YOUR FEARS AND FOUND YOUR footing, the only thing left for you to do to officially overcome fear is to focus on your future. It's one thing to overcome fear in a moment or even during a season of life, but to make overcoming fear a lifestyle, you must make your way forward. You must point yourself squarely toward the future.

I talked a little bit about this in the last chapter when I shared about my core value of integrity. Because I want to live an authentic life, I regularly push myself beyond my comfort zone and into new territory. I'm always looking at what's next, where I can go, and how I can dream bigger dreams than the ones I'm currently living out. I do that because it helps me keep my fear in check by giving me something greater to live for. There's a lot of power in a genuine dream. You can call it a vision, a purpose, or a mission, but the end result is the same: it motivates you to take one more step forward on your journey than you thought possible . . . and I promise it is one more step than most other people will take. Anyone can tap into tremendous energy just by living life according to their values and dreams.

I mentioned earlier that I was troubled as a young man by the financial struggles that my family and others in the circus business went through. In her book, *The Last of the Wallendas*, my mother wrote that the industry was dying, but I came to realize it wasn't dying; it was changing.

People and performances that once belonged solely under the big top were finding outlets in other places. I noticed that a lot of traditional circus acts were trying something different, and there was no better example than in the world of magic. David Copperfield, Criss Angel, David Blaine, and other prominent magicians became better known as "performers" once they started hosting television specials; then they leveraged that popularity to host showcases of their own, often in places like Las Vegas, where they weren't just part of the act; they *were* the act. I could see that the culture treated them differently when they weren't under the big top. They weren't just performers; they were icons that fans would flock to see because of what they could create for the audience: that sense of magic and amazement that was vanishing from the circus.

I remember looking at performers like that and thinking, *I do something that's unique to very few people in the world. Why can't I do that too? What limits me from making that transition?* I started dreaming about how I could become the best-known wire walker in the world, a name that everyone around the globe would know because of my skill in my unique area. I knew I would have to literally move out from beneath the big top to make that happen, and I wrestled with that idea. I've grown up loving the circus—it is not just part of my background; it is my birthright. But I knew if I wanted to help the circus survive, I would have to help it change—and if I wanted the influence to help it change, I would have to build that influence outside the ring.

So I set out to do what Copperfield and Angel and others had done—I went in pursuit of television partners who would help me build my brand.

THE ROAD TO REDEMPTION

As I began to push toward my dreams, I knew there would be some resistance. Everything I do—everything I've always done—is a circus act, but when I took my act out of the ring, it had to be changed in some ways to make it accessible. And the same changes that made me more relatable to the audience were the changes that offended some circus purists. The road I chose to walk didn't sit well with some from that world because on the face of it, it looked like I was betraying the community and people I loved.

The best example I can give you comes down to a simple pair of blue jeans. Not too long after I secured my Grand Canyon special, I made the decision to wear jeans during the broadcast. Now, jeans aren't necessarily the most comfortable thing to walk a wire in, but since I was looking to connect with my audience, I knew that when I was on that wire in front of the camera, I had to be relatable to the viewer. Once that detail came to light, however, I was instantly an outcast in some parts of the circus community. How could I possibly wear jeans rather than sequins and rhinestones or pink tights? That's a little bit of a joke, but the reality is, some people expected me to keep that part of the tradition of a circus act alive. To them, it was an essential part of the circus. I consciously chose not to wear a circus costume because if I did, I wouldn't have the following I have. The viewers of that TV special might not completely relate to my walking on a wire, but they still feel comfortable with me because I look just like any other guy out walking in jeans.

It's just not as easy to relate to a guy wearing sequins and rhinestones.

I can't tell you how difficult a choice this was for me, and I'm not just saying that. I didn't want to be alienated from the people I loved or be seen as someone who was somehow hurting the circus in any way. But I also knew that what I was doing was for a purpose—everything was with my larger dream in mind.

What was that larger dream? To one day open my own circus and do things differently; to redeem something meaningful to me and my family. It's been the constant theme of my career, and I can't ever get away from that desire to take what was so precious to me growing up—my family, our legacy, and our industry—and give it new life. But the costs are real, and they are painful, so the fallout over the jeans—as minor as it was—still hurt me. In fact, the reality is I probably *would* have worn rhinestones if not for Erendira.

When we were dating, we would often have conversations about the need to change the industry in some way, and she brought those talks back to mind as I wrestled over the jeans. She helped me refocus on the larger purpose—that I was expanding my world in order to preserve it—and encouraged me to push forward to do my art and share my passion on a bigger scale.

Does this resonate with you? Are there places in your life where you feel a need for change or maybe a shift in how you pursue the life you want? If so, what's preventing you from making those changes? Maybe you feel the way I did—that making those changes would somehow hurt the people you care about or would cost you relationships you hold dear. Those are very real challenges that dreamers face every day, and often people settle for a crushed dream instead of upsetting their relationship dynamics. That may be the right choice—for that moment—but sometimes it's only fear that keeps us from making those changes. I felt fear as I stepped out on my own, and it was significant. But fear cannot win out over our dreams, or else we end up doing what everyone before us always did. It takes courage to pioneer. It takes faith to step out into your dreams—and to continue stepping out. After all, you don't always achieve your dream on the first shot. It takes a process to get there, and that process costs you something. That's where so many people get stuck: they don't want the journey; they want the destination. And when the process takes longer than expected or the price is higher than they imagined, most people get bogged down. As a result, they give up on their dreams, often just before they break wide open.

It's like sitting in traffic—when I'm driving, I have to keep in mind that there will be challenges along the way. If I don't remind myself of the delays I'm likely to experience, then when I get stuck at a red light or in traffic, I easily get frustrated, feeling like *I've got to get moving!* I'll view the delay as a punishment or an obstacle or a sign that the universe is unfair.

But what if the reason I'm stuck at the traffic light isn't because the world is unjust but because there was a collision waiting for me if I made it through that light?

Whether we're talking about traffic or our dreams, we often feel like a pause is a problem instead of a necessary part of the process. Because of that, I think we give up on our dreams too easily and overlook God's power to work on our behalf. Maybe that pause is there for a reason. Maybe it's to redirect our steps to a better, more effective way to fulfill our dreams. I believe God is looking out for us, if we will look for God in that situation. It's like with Lijana's fall—after getting past the initial shock, I realized that if my sister had died, I likely would have still gotten back on a wire one day in her honor. I would have brought good out of it because I know that's what she would have wanted, and it's what my family and my ancestors would want too.

For some people, that was too hard to accept. They felt like, had Lijana died, giving up the wire would have been the only sensible thing to do. But that's not how we're wired—and I'm not just talking about my family. Think about it: We all know that many people die in car accidents each year, but how many of those family members give up driving? They all eventually get back in the car and drive! It's human nature, and yet I've been attacked sometimes by people who say, "How stupid are you to get back on that wire? That should've been your wake-up call!" And it was, but what I woke up to wasn't regret. It was joy, because Lijana not only lived; she walked the wire with me in Times Square, thank God!

We all get knocked down. But what will help you get into a car after a car accident or onto an airplane after news of an airplane crash is the same thing that will move you forward toward any dream: your passion for what you love to do. That passion is what motivates you, what keeps you focused on the future, but you must choose to follow it.

After all, God created us with free will. We're not robots. He could have made us without free will, and we would all worship him every day and everything would be just perfect, but we wouldn't be leading lives. To truly live, we must use our free will, and as long as we have free will, we will all make mistakes. I want to live with the understanding that there's potential for good in everything that happens to us, and we can find it as long as we get back up after we get knocked down. God created us to be *over*achievers, not *under*achievers. He doesn't want us to give up; he wants us to keep going.

I know that's a lot to take in, but how many people have passions they give up because of a setback? I want to encourage them—encourage you—that when these things happen, there's a bigger opportunity within each negative situation. The good might not be apparent, but it is there. Lijana's fall was the worst situation I'd dealt with to that point in my life, and we were still able to use it to inspire, encourage, and uplift others and get them through falls of their own.

For me, that's what it's about.

Let me put it this way: I won't say that I know everything happens for a purpose, but I will say that everything that happens is purposeless unless we make it a point to *find* a purpose in it. That's why I'm continuing my journey to chase my dreams: it gives me a purpose, which keeps me passionate. The road I'm on isn't just about me; it's about redefining for the world what they can expect from my community, to remind them that the circus isn't just about entertainment; it's about magic. That's why I pushed through that initial discomfort about the jeans. It's why I went from the Grand Canyon to Niagara Falls to Times Square. I needed to do those things so I could build a brand strong enough to come back to my heritage, back to the big top, and do so having changed the conversation and expectations around the circus.

BREATHING LIFE INTO A DYING INDUSTRY

I went to a circus not too long ago called UniverSoul Circus, and what makes it unique is that it's an African American circus. The man who owns it was a promoter for Motown, and the circus is based in Atlanta, though they tour all over. My wife's cousin Danny Rodriguez runs the show, so we went one night when they were performing in Sarasota. It was under a big top, and it was the most exciting, fun, and uplifting show. We had an incredible time.

I was like, "Man, how can I do this?" And even though I wasn't the target audience, the whole time I was into it; I was excited. What amazed me was there was a lot of production without a lot of cost—there were points where they were just throwing a bunch of big beach balls around the audience. Some of the old, traditional acts were really expensive to bring from Europe, but this show stayed true to its vision. It ended up being more about production, but it just *worked*.

When I left, I left excited because my dream had been inspired.

But I also left feeling afraid.

I'm at the stage of my career where opening a circus of my own is no longer just a dream. My brand is still growing, but I'm at a place where I could easily pull together the financing on my own. It would be an expensive proposition—nearly $2.5 million just for a tent—but if I wanted to, I could make my dream a reality. I don't have all of the details worked out, but I've thought a lot about what I would need to do. I would need to hire someone without a circus background to help me produce it—maybe someone from Broadway who understands the magic of performance but sees through a different lens. I would need to secure a good home base where we could set up and begin working for the first few years, a place where there would be an appreciation for the type of circus I would create. I would need to find the next generation of talent, a new era of performers who would captivate and amaze the audience with their skills and abilities. Then we would need to put together a show that absolutely mesmerizes everyone, from a child to a teen to an adult. We would have to create a circus that people haven't experienced in years.

That's a massive task. After all, there have been people over the years who have tried to reinvent the circus—one of the most famous being Cirque du Soleil. You've probably heard of them and maybe have even seen one of their performances; they've performed in front of 180 million people in sixty countries around the world.[1] Cirque began in Canada in the early 1980s when a group of street performers formed a troupe near Quebec City. They were mostly stilt walkers and other street performers, but they worked hard at their craft and developed a traveling show that went across Canada in 1984 to celebrate the 450th anniversary of the country's discovery. The beauty and magic of their production resonated with people, and in 1987 they launched their first US tour. The show was a hit—amazing music, gorgeous costumes, incredible performers—and quickly became a phenomenon. They eventually launched a residency in Las Vegas (a show called *Mystère*) and began rolling out shows featuring different themes.[2] In 2015, an investment firm purchased a majority stake in the company for $1.5 billion.

Cirque is what you could call a success story. In fact, you could call it a *wildly* successful story. I should look at Cirque and feel confident about my dream because these performers proved that so many of the concepts I've been thinking about my entire life are not only viable; they're what people want. It would seem like a no-brainer for me to follow their example as a blueprint for my own show. Except in March 2020, Cirque filed for debt restructuring relief, including the possibility of bankruptcy.[3] After the coronavirus outbreak forced governments to forbid gatherings of more than ten to fifty people, Cirque had to shut down. The owners laid off the majority of their four-thousand-person staff and began working with creditors to figure out their $900 million debt.[4] As I write this, no one knows how the story will play out, but it's another sad chapter in the history of the circus and has some people wondering if the industry is all but done.

I remember asking the same question when Ringling Brothers first began talking about shutting its doors. I wondered if my dream of owning a circus was in jeopardy, because the closing of Ringling would have to be seen as a signal that the industry was fading. But the more I thought about it, the more I became convinced that it wasn't a signal that the industry was dying; it was a signal that the industry needed to evolve. To grow. To change. I still feel the same way, even after reading the news about Cirque. There's still room for the magic of our industry, still a place for us to touch hearts and inspire imaginations. To do that, however, I have to learn the lessons from Ringling and Cirque and keep living out the lessons from this book.

I have to push myself back to what I wrote earlier in this chapter—there's good in every situation if we look for it. Yes, there's risk with launching my own circus; yes, there's fear; but there's also the joy of staying in front of my fears.

That's where I want to be: ahead of my fears. I don't want to give in to them or be overwhelmed by them; I want to be out in front of them, finding the positive in them so I can continue stretching myself to be the best person I can be. When fear is ahead of you, it is a roadblock. When fear is behind you, it is an energizer, and that's good. It can help you do things no one ever thought possible. In the next two chapters, I want to tell you how my fear helped me do what sounded impossible—and do it on live TV. I want to tell you about my walk across an active volcano.

CHAPTER 12

WHEN OVERCOMERS GET OVERWHELMED

ONE OF THE TOUGHEST THINGS ABOUT FACING FEAR is that the process never ends. The second you have tackled one fear, another is there waiting. It's like that Whac-A-Mole game at the county fair!

We live in a broken world, and that means things rarely work the way we plan or expect. Even after you discipline yourself to face your fears, find your footing, and focus on your future, there are still going to be moments when you are simply overwhelmed. When this happens, it's easy to get down on yourself. You know what you need to do but struggle to apply the lessons, and then discouragement comes along and makes you feel even worse. Throughout my career, I've experienced this sort of thing time and time again, so much so that I've come to really appreciate the power behind something Jesus said to his disciples in

John 16: "In this world you will have trouble. But take heart! I have overcome the world" (v. 33).

I leaned into that verse a lot in 2019 and 2020. In addition to working on this book and working my way through the whole process of overcoming fear, I was simultaneously working on the most dangerous wire walk of my career. On March 4, 2020, in a special broadcast live on ABC, I walked 1,800 feet across the open mouth of the Masaya volcano in Nicaragua. It is one of the world's most active volcanoes, with molten lava bubbling up constantly from its center. Nothing I've ever done can even come close to matching the intensity and danger of that walk, which is why I can look back now and say that I should've expected the trouble that came my way. I should have known that a walk that big, that audacious, would draw as many attacks from Satan as possible. But I was a bit fooled, because the problems I encountered weren't the usual big problems that crop up early with this kind of stunt.

The time leading up to an event like this is always busy, and busyness can of course be overwhelming. There's all of the media requirements and all of the meetings and phone calls. Maybe there's a challenge with booking hotel rooms or a struggle to effectively manage the shipping manifest for the equipment. And I haven't even mentioned the time it takes to finalize plans with all the various agencies and partners involved in a production like this. There are many details that have to be checked and rechecked, but just a few weeks before showtime, I felt like everything was falling into place step by step. For a time, I thought I had beaten fear.

But that's when the problems began cropping up.

Here's the thing about problems: when they come one at a time, they're easy to handle. They can be inconvenient, sure, but once you find solutions and move past them, they become just a memory. But when problems cascade—when a bunch of things start going wrong all at once—it doesn't take much for that to trigger a fear snowball, one huge anxiety you can't control.

That's exactly what happened to me. As I began my training, I decided to shift my thinking. I mentioned in chapter 10 that I never get on a wire thinking, *Gosh, this is easy!* For most of my career, I've tried to think about the worst possible scenario so I could prepare myself for it—no matter how unlikely it might be. But as I started training for Masaya, my mindset was different; the hard work of facing my fears after the Sarasota accident and learning to grow through that process was starting to pay dividends. I think part of it was a realization of how tired that negative approach was making me; how I was doing damage to my own psyche by constantly thinking about worst-case scenarios. So I made the decision to begin visualizing myself walking on the best wire of my career. I began asking myself, *What would happen if things went well? What if the winds at the center of the volcano weren't that bad?*

As a result, my first few training sessions went incredibly well. Thinking positive—and staying positive—translated into my practice and allowed me to accelerate my program a bit. Soon, however, I started having a bunch of pains in my knee and ankle, pains that I hadn't felt in a long time. I figured it was the sort of thing that came with age, so while it was annoying, I knew I would just have to work through it. I'd have to take care of myself and not get too much in my head whenever I felt a small twinge of pain, or else I'd run the risk of turning a molehill into a mountain. I should have kept that in mind not just for myself but for my wife as well. It would have spared her a lot of pain—and spared all of us a lot of anxiety.

A PAIN IN THE LEG

A few months before the walk, we decided that Erendira would open the show dangling from a lyra under a helicopter. My wife would essentially hang by her toes on a hoop attached to the bottom of a helicopter, all while performing beautiful aerial ballet. The act would culminate with her hanging by nothing but her teeth. We added this performance not only to showcase my wife and her amazing skills but to create extra interest for the viewers.

In early February, about a month before the special, my broadcast partners at Dick Clark Productions sent a film crew to Sarasota to shoot some packages of us training. These short clips would be used to take viewers behind the scenes at different points during the broadcast to help them understand how we prepared for these performances. Even though we knew Erendira would be on the lyra under the helicopter, we didn't want to spoil the surprise for the viewers. So when the film crew arrived, we agreed we weren't going to show anything she was actually doing. That meant we had to come up with other ideas, so one of the crew members said, "Why don't we do something to sweeten this part of the package? Why don't you guys do a pyramid on the wire with her on top?"

We talked it over, and a simple pyramid was something we knew we could do with zero problems. As we made our way to the wire, Erendira pulled me aside and said, "I'm going to do a split."

We'd done this hundreds of times before, so I said, "Great!"

We got up on the wire, and everything was going well until we got out into the middle. Right when Erendira should've revealed her big trick, she did nothing. She didn't do the split.

Once we got to the opposite platform, I asked her, "Why didn't you do the split?"

"It just didn't feel right. I felt like I shouldn't do it."

Granted, we were doing a trick we hadn't really prepared for, and even though we're seasoned pros, it had still been a while since she'd done this trick out on the wire. I could tell she was uncomfortable, but it seemed silly. So I decided to give her a little tough love.

"You need to stop letting it get into your head," I told her. "You need to do the split."

We reset for another take, letting the camera crews adjust angles and everything, and the second time we went out, Erendira said again, "I don't feel comfortable."

"Stop letting it get into your head!" I hissed. "We're in the middle of the wire. You need to do the split."

Erendira nodded, and as she went down into her split, she suddenly felt an incredible pain in her leg. I know when my wife is truly in pain, and I knew immediately we had to get down from the wire and get her some help. I literally carried her to the car and rushed her to a friend of ours, Dr. David Sugar, who is an orthopedic surgeon. Even though it was after-hours when we called him, he stayed in his office late so we could get her examined. After X-rays and a CT scan, our friend came back with his diagnosis.

"It's a torn hamstring, which means two to three months of recovery time. You've got to take it easy. You can't do much, and you certainly can't train."

A torn hamstring with a month to go before the special. It was miserable news, and I felt horrible. Even though Erendira told me she was uncomfortable, I pushed her through what I thought was a mental block, and she suffered for it. She told me later she believed the unease she felt was the Holy Spirit saying to her, *Don't do it*. And there I was saying she should!

It was a difficult hurdle thrown our way, and we still had the film crew there for more shooting. We didn't tell anyone what was going on, even though they were filming. I don't think to this day they fully realized the magnitude of Erendira's injury. She couldn't walk at first, which made her very upset. We didn't know what to do besides pray about it. Luckily, she is extremely healthy; as a vegetarian, she eats really well, so she adjusted her diet to include a healthy vegetable juice in the morning. After about ten days she began recovering, and she was back to practice soon after that. By the time the special aired on March 4, she was 90 percent recovered.

But you can see how the cascade started, with her injury being the first setback; that exhibition of her skill on live television was something she was so excited about, something she really wanted to do. If that had been the only setback, it would've been enough. But during this same window, we had an issue with a shipping container for some of our gear. We had to get the rigging down to Nicaragua well in advance of the special to see how everything would hold up over the volcano, and we ran into challenges getting some of the containers down there. It was a problem, but it was happening far enough out that it was an inconvenience more than a major concern.

While that was happening, I was upping my training by adding in all the safety equipment we felt I would need for the walk. The Masaya volcano spits out an enormous amount of sulfuric gases and ash, which meant I wouldn't be able to walk across without my face being covered or without emergency oxygen. I was doing my best to get prepared physically and mentally, walking up to a mile a day on the wire while wearing an oxygen tank with a gas mask, along with a weighted harness on my chest. So in the middle of some of my hardest, most tedious training, I was dealing with shipping-container issues while nursing an injured wife.

Long story short, I was reacting so well that I felt like my psyche was borderline bulletproof. My rehearsal wire was very loose, so I knew if I could handle myself on that one, I'd be more than prepared for the stabler wire over the volcano. Mentally and physically, I felt strong. I was punching fear in the face. More good news: most of the gear was on the ground, and the rigging team was getting the wire strung up across the volcano's mouth. My dad was scheduled to go down near the end of February and oversee the rigging process for me. The cascade of problems seemed to be slowing.

ISSUES WITH THE WIRE

"Nik, we have a major concern."

My dad was down in Nicaragua for his inspection, and he had called me on the phone. Mind you, I told my team I didn't want to hear anything negative once they got down there. I only wanted to hear positive things because I needed to keep my mind in a positive place. As they loaded to head south, I had given them all—Dad included—one last instruction: "Don't tell me the bad stuff happening down there. You're the best, and you're there for one purpose. Whatever happens, just figure things out."

I hoped that would be the case, but this was my dad saying, "We have a problem." Suddenly my mind accelerated a million miles an hour in every wrong direction. Dad laid out the situation for me: the riggers had run a rope across the center of the volcano to help them set up the wire. Overnight they left two carabiners—little circle clips used in mountain climbing—in the middle of their rope, and when Dad and the team reeled them in, they noticed that the carabiners were covered in a greasy substance.

"We don't know what it is," he said. "We're not really sure what's going on, but for some reason it appears that the volcano is emitting some sort of greasy substance that none of us can figure out."

Our team had studied the Masaya volcano for nearly

two years at that point, so what my dad was saying made *no* sense—not scientifically, anyway. "Dad, I don't get it. What are we dealing with?"

"We don't know. We're going to have to do a bunch more research."

I was irritated. "Dad, I told you I didn't want to hear bad news. This is bad news."

"I know," he said, "but as your father, I can't *not* tell you. You need to train and prepare for this. Me and Uncle Mike, we're going to work on the problem, and we'll see what we can figure out."

He called me the next day. "The good news is we don't think it's necessarily grease, but it's certainly a very slippery substance. There appears to be high levels of humidity mixing with the gas and some small particles in the air that the volcano is emitting. It creates this very fine dust that feels and looks just like grease. I sent you a picture."

My phone dinged as the picture came in. He was right—it did look just like grease.

"Okay," I said. "What next?"

"Here's what I want you to do—I want you to go online and buy some bags of sand that they use for rock tumbling, the kind used to clean up stones and stuff. Buy that, sprinkle it on the wire, spray it down with some water, and walk on that."

"Dad, that doesn't make sense. I don't think that's going to do anything for me."

He said, "Well, I don't know what else to tell you. We'll keep working."

The next night they stayed late. They brought some

high-wattage lights that allowed them to use binoculars to examine the middle of the wire. The wire was literally dripping, almost as if it were melting. When Dad called, he said, "It looks like the wire at Niagara Falls—it's just covered in this substance, all in the middle of the wire."

By this point, I was not sleeping at all. Days of uncertainty about the wire and what was causing the weird substance—let alone how that substance might affect my walk—meant no possibility of sleep whatsoever.

The next morning, I woke up and did something I've never done before. I went into my bathroom cupboard, grabbed a giant jar of Vaseline, and went out to my rehearsal wire. I marked off one area about fifteen feet long and I covered it in Vaseline.

Then I started walking on it back and forth.

At that point, we were just weeks away from the show, so I was fully committed; there was no turning back. I had to figure out how I was going to walk on a cable covered in grease, so I started training on a fully greased wire. It actually went well, and I quickly learned that the grease wouldn't really affect me aside from my traction. Since the wire at the volcano wasn't too steep, I wasn't overly concerned with traction.

I ended up training on that wire quite a bit. Day after day I felt better and even started to feel confident. But every time I started to feel good, more little things would crop up. I'm always very sensitive before my walks anyway, but the mounting pressure wasn't helping. I was out to dinner one night, and someone at a table near me said something with the word *fall* in it—something like, "I love fall; it's my favorite season." As soon as I heard "fall," my heart immediately started racing. I didn't want to hear that word come out of anyone's mouth, even if they just happened to be around me. Casual conversation was now bothering me!

The cascade was in full effect. Basically, my mind was eaten up with worry—so when my dad called me to tell me of another challenge, I mentally fell off a cliff. There were so many things that kept adding up; it seemed like bad news kept coming and coming and coming, so I pulled out my phone and captured what I was thinking.

I want to share these raw thoughts with you to help you understand how easily fear can overwhelm a person, even someone who has worked so hard to overcome it. Here's what I wrote:

February 20 9:19 PM

My dad calls and says he is going out on the wire right to the middle via the rigging carts, to see how bad the conditions may be.

He tells me he will call me as soon as he gets back in to let me know how it is. He then says we have concerns of heat tubes and says he has to go!

I'm at Cheesecake Factory in Sarasota after a long day of media interviews and meetings and practicing on the wire. A very windy day of practice on the wire.

My feet are sore from all of the practice.

My mind starts to torment me. Heat tubes? What is a heat tube? Is the wire going to be hot? Did we somehow miss something in our studies leading up to this point? I'm now less than 2 weeks out. How will I prepare? What will I have to wear? Are my shoes going to protect my feet? I already ordered food prior to the call, but I can't eat. It sucks, since I don't want my family to see the war raging in my head. How can I fake that I am fine? They don't need to worry. This is an issue I have to deal with. What good does worry do for me, let alone them?

We finish dinner and I get my food packed up. We are heading home for the night. The entire 25-minute car ride home I am waiting for my dad to call. Please God let him bring me good news. Please God. Dear Jesus. God, I really need good news!

And the phone is silent. 30 minutes go by; surely he should have called by now. 45 minutes go by. Something must be terribly wrong! Don't be stupid; control your thoughts. 1 hour goes by; it's really bad, I know it! Control your thoughts! 1:15 goes by; my mind is racing. I decide to shower and play Bethel's "Raise a Hallelujah." Trying to sing louder than the horrible thoughts racing through my mind. 2 hours go by. I'm freaking out. Every single bad thought of the worst case scenarios is eating me alive. I feel like I am being choked, I feel like I am being tormented . . . I feel like I am being an idiot. God has always been there for me. He has never let me down, but like the Israelites I just can't seem to learn to just trust in him. Every walk I've done he has been there! They start out with a hailstorm leading up to the walk, but he always delivers, yet I still lack faith.

As I lay in bed waiting for a report back from my earthly father I began to lack trust in my heavenly Father. It's an emotional roller coaster with stress levels like I've never experienced before. From stressful news of an oily wire to better news that it seems to be sandy not oily, back to concerns of heat to great news report on the conditions in the middle of the wire.

I lay waiting and in an emotional battle, a war in my head! I began to "sing a little louder," but sadly it wasn't loud enough, so I began to read the Word, and that wasn't easing the gunfire. I began to come against the attacks of Satan in Jesus' name and cast out the thoughts burning holes in my heart. I fought and fought and fought and praised and worshiped and prayed and read. My mind was in my control and no one other than myself.

Finally my wife says just text him, but she doesn't know I already did, and he didn't respond—only adding fuel to my emotional fire.

I decide I will text him on WhatsApp since he is international: "Did you make it back to the hotel?"

It's 11:26 p.m.

I see he reads the text but nothing for what seems like an eternity, but then after 90 seconds he responds.

"On my way back now."

Now my heart is racing at 900 mph. What does he have to say? Is it good? Is it bad? I start asking him questions.

At this point, I want to share with you the text chain with my dad. He spent two hours on the edge of an active volcano doing everything he could to get me every answer he could. Looking back at this now, I can feel the anxiety in my words, and the comfort and peace in his. But in those moments, I was literally unaware of either.

> Me: Okay. Were you able to check the wire?
>
> **Him: Yes.**
>
> The middle?
>
> **Yes.**
>
> How was it?
>
> **Super.**
>
> Did the gas mask work?
>
> **Very well.**
>
> Praise God. What about the goggles?
>
> **Goggles were great.**
>
> Heat?
>
> **Mild and occasional blasts.
> Feels like hot for a few seconds,
> then fine, and then cool.**
>
> What's the experience in the
> crater, around the edge?
> Moisture?
>
> **Yes. But don't think it will
> affect your grip at all.**
>
> So all in all, do you feel better?
>
> **Yes. Big gusts of wind in your
> face, but not so bad.**
>
> That's what I practiced in today in Sarasota!

Good practice.

Thank God for that great news.

Amen. He is in charge.

Were you able to remove the gas mask?

That's a no go.

Oxygen tanks?

**We weren't doing anything
physical, we were fine.**

This is all such encouraging news.
After a rough start to the day, thank you, Jesus.
Happy you went out there yourself.
Really, really helped my confidence
and comfort level.
Thank you so much.

**Love you, my son. You're a
blessing to the Lord.**

I don't know why God chose me, but
I know he will get all the glory.

I picked up my phone and finished typing my thoughts
into my note:

What did I learn? I learned that God supplies
ALL of my needs. ALL of them. He even supplies my
emotional needs. Why do I continually have to go
through these battles? When will I learn that he is in full
control and just rest in that? I feel foolish, I feel dumb, I
feel immature. And then I realize I am just human.

My only thought is that through these battles I
will become stronger in my faith. My God supplies all

of my needs. I trust yet I doubt, I know yet I forget, I try yet I still fail.

When I put my phone down, I felt relieved. After two hours of worrying, I finally had my answers, which meant I could continue with my training in a better frame of mind. The fears I'd been dragging around had been met with facts. With no uncertainty to play with, they began to disappear. I found out later on that it took my dad only about thirty minutes to do the inspection. He was able to go down, check everything, check it again, and then head back to the hotel. To this day, I'm not sure why it took him so long to get back to me—I think, since the news was good, he didn't feel that rushed to tell me.

After all, there was nothing to worry about—for him!

For me, however, those two hours were agony. And yet God provided answers in the end. He took care of me, like he always does, and I knew that I would need to keep that truth in mind in order to complete the walk.

This lesson is true for many of us. We forget that our fear solves nothing. Matthew 6:27 asks, "Can any one of you by worrying add a single hour to your life?"

Our actions can change the outcome, but our fears cannot. There were still plenty of concerns—wires dripping with water, gases in the air, humidity in the air—but knowing that someone I trusted had checked things out gave me hope. I wouldn't be able to breeze through the walk—I would still have to focus on each and every step to make my footing sure—but at least I had more information to help me go back to my training with increased confidence.

But still, as the day of the walk drew closer, my human nature wanted to drag my mind to dark places, and I struggled back and forth between feeling good and feeling worried.

I needed to get myself together. I needed more focus on heavenly wisdom.

CHAPTER 13

FRESH STEPS OF FAITH

THE WEEK OF FEBRUARY 24 WAS MY BIG MEDIA TOUR. I flew to New York midweek for some press, including stops at *Good Morning America* and *LIVE with Kelly and Ryan*. I enjoyed talking about the special, but I flew back home with only two days of final intense training to refocus and make late adjustments. I pushed myself to train really, really hard both days and fell into bed exhausted that Saturday night.

The family and I flew down to Managua, the capital of Nicaragua, on Sunday, March 1. The moment we landed, I was whisked away—skipping customs and everything—because of some chaos at the airport. Apparently, a Nicaraguan boxer had won a major championship the night before and was coming into the airport around the same time I was. Due to concerns over crowds, a security team put me in a car, and I received a police escort at ninety miles an hour out of the airport and away from the area. It happened so fast I didn't even get a chance to check in with my family—they were left behind while I was hustled away. As our motorcade neared the hotel, I had the chance to call and check on them and was relieved when they said they were fine and would see me at the hotel. They were just grateful to know that I was okay too.

After settling in, I began feeling pretty good. We were only a few days away from the walk, and despite some challenges, everything seemed to be on track. I felt physically and mentally prepared, confident that I was fully ready to tackle this walk. In fact, I felt more than confident; I felt strong.

After getting adjusted to the room, I called my dad and invited him to come up so we could talk. As we were sitting there chatting, he asked if I was scared about the condition of the wire, and I told him I wasn't. He reassured me that the wire was going to be great, nice and tight. All the words I wanted to hear. Dad was being so positive, which was helping me continue to relax, and the time together was perfect.

Then, out of the blue he got a message on his phone, and his tone changed. "We have a big problem," he said, barely looking up from his phone.

Three days out. I was ready to go and feeling good. And then I wasn't. Before he said another word, my mind began to reel. Dad stepped out of the room, then back a few minutes later.

"We have a problem with the stabilizer wires. They're snapping."

"What? What are you saying?"

"The stabilizer wires are snapping, Nik."

We both were immediately sure that they were snapping

as a result of the gas, but why were they snapping now, when we tested the same wires for three weeks in the same location months prior to the walk and had no issues? Why were the gases stronger now than they had been when we tested them? When we chose those wires for the stabilizers, our research told us they were rated five times stronger than what was necessary. What changed?

It is my preference that every wire I walk on has stabilization wires to help keep the main wire steady under my feet. Stabilizers are often challenging to run, given the places I've walked across, but I've never had stabilizers snap on me before.

We would have to go to the site and examine everything in order to get answers. Again, my mental state was shaken. Instead of being able to simply relax, visualize the walk, and get my focus where it needed to be, I was going to be neck-deep in solving a problem I had never experienced before.

Unlike a lot of other artists or performers, I don't just show up on the day of a stunt and do my thing—I'm intimately involved in every prewalk detail, from the packing to the shipping to the rigging and the entire production setup. It's just part of my nature. While this allows me to ensure that I give every walk nothing but my best, it also opens me up to significant challenges. When you're involved in almost everything, you understand how bad things are when problems arise. And the more you know, the more that knowledge weighs on you.

So instead of concentrating on my walk, I was in problem-solving mode because we had wires that were in danger. My dad was able to learn that the center stabilizers were the issue, which meant the problem was even more significant: How in the world would we get to the middle to make repairs if they were unstable? When the stabilizers are installed, they begin at the main wire's center and then work toward either end. Because of that process, there's no simple way of getting back to the middle of the wire to make corrections or repairs. Beyond that, we were three days away from the show—and we were in Central America. If we had to replace each cable entirely, where would we get the wire we needed? It would take almost twenty-five miles of new cable to replace all of the stabilizers if they were corroded, and getting that much cable shipped to where we were, plus getting it installed correctly, would never happen in three days. It was simply impossible.

What were we going to do?

BIG PROBLEMS, SMALL SOLUTIONS

My mental spiral turned into a free fall rather quickly as I tried to control things so far beyond my control. I could feel the fear of uncertainty creeping in, and with it came the questions of doubt. *Why is this happening? Isn't this what God has called me to do? How in the world am I going to handle this?* I had to pause my problem-solving for a moment and come back to those things I knew were true: everything that happens, God can make something good from. Even though things were beyond my control, they weren't beyond his—I just had to surrender myself again to that fact and trust him to show me the way.

My team needed answers, so we sent one of the riggers out to the site, and he was able to determine why the center cables were snapping: to get those particular cables installed, they had to put a hard bend into them, and that bend, the rigger believed, was causing the braided cable to open up. With the different strands of the cable exposed, the volcano's gases and humidity were able to soak into the center of that wire row, causing the entire run to fail prematurely. So now we had the good news—we knew why and where the cables were failing—but we still hadn't dealt with the bad news: we'd have to re-rig the entire wire unless we came up with a different plan.

When I don't have answers, I start praying, so even as the rest of the team began discussing options, I was asking God to give me wisdom on how to fix the problem.

For some reason, when I was shipping everything over, I included a bunch of these things called Crosby clips—tiny wire rope clips. I don't know why I did it; it's not like they're part of the regular packing manifesto, but I guess I decided to send them in the crates just in case. As I was praying, these clips came to mind, and I could see a possible plan taking shape. God was in control.

When I came back to my team, they were planning on rigging a wire cart beneath the main wire, pulling out to the compromised section, and trying to recrimp the wire at 1,800 feet in the air. The other option was unhooking the cables from the ground, recrimping them, and then reconnecting them. The tensioners in the crater were already seizing up from the gases eating away at them, and we only had a few days to do this. Keep in mind, it took the team over a week to install them in the first place. The odds were against us, and the pressure for success was too high for me to be confident in either plan. I said, "Here's a different idea. Can someone check to see if I packed those Crosby clips?"

"I think so, yeah," Dieter said.

"All right. Do we have them here?"

After a quick look around the camp, we were able to find them. My dad looked at me and said, "What are you thinking?"

"I'm thinking we can use the Crosby clips and add a short length of new cable to bypass the compromised section of the stabilizers, so even if they fail, they won't move, because the clips will keep them in place. If anything, they might move half an inch or so, but they're not going to whiplash and fall down into the crater. I think it could work."

The team agreed, and they immediately went to work. It was truly spectacular what they did, working thirty-six hours over the next two days to get it done. They didn't finish repairing those cables until the morning of the walk. We had a solution we were confident would work if time allowed. We could move forward with the performance. The show would go on, and it would be even more meaningful knowing that we'd overcome such a massive setback with just days to spare.

Things were looking a bit brighter. In fact, after such long days on Sunday and Monday, I needed something different. On Monday night I asked one of my friends, Dan Minor, to bring his guitar to our hotel room and play some of my favorite praise and worship songs. It was relief for my troubled mind, so we did it again on Tuesday night, all of us enjoying a time of Bible study and worship. But in the middle of our time together, I got a text from one of the executive producers on the show: "We need to talk. Right away."

I excused myself and went out into the hall so I could call the producer back. I wasn't sure what could be so urgent, given that the wire problem was being resolved, but when he answered, he said they were in the middle of rehearsal and they needed me at the site. Keep in mind, I'd already been out at the site that day working on the wire, and as a general rule, I don't like visiting the site less than twenty-four hours before showtime. If I could arrive on-site, put my wire shoes on, and get on the wire, it would be the best thing in the world for me mentally. I'd much rather just perform with no time to think about it. Add in my exhaustion—I hadn't slept much Monday night, either—and I knew it wasn't helpful for me to go out there that night.

I told the producer I couldn't come and asked him to include one of my team members in whatever was happening so I could be filled in. The newest challenge was connected to Erendira's part of the show, which the production team was suggesting needed to be canceled. Remember, the plan was that before I walked over the volcano, Erendira would fly over the lava in a helicopter and dangle from a lyra.

As the crew was doing its walk-through, simulating the show, they placed sandbags in the helicopter where my wife would sit. "Basically, the winds are so bad that it took over ten minutes just to get off the ground," the producer said. "And when the pilot went to hover above the volcano, it was so rough that the lyra with the sandbags kept smacking the bottom of the helicopter."

"So what are you saying?" I asked.

"We can't do this stunt. The winds are too unpredictable. There's no way they can fly."

Now, my pilot had been there three weeks earlier and had taken the helicopter over the volcano. We leave nothing to chance when we prepare; we are methodical and meticulous, and we wanted to be certain that every stunt can work. And it did—for *us*. But that night during the network rehearsal, out of nowhere the winds were so rough that the helicopter couldn't fly. It was beyond my control—not just because nature was acting out but because the network ultimately got to make that call. As a good partner, I understood their reasoning, but I was still sideswiped by the reality. My skin went clammy and I went pale, not only because I had to tell my wife that she couldn't perform, but because I started thinking that I had to *walk* in winds that a helicopter coudn't *fly* in.

In one phone call, everything had gone completely sideways. The producer said the winds were so insane, so unpredictable, so vicious that a flying machine couldn't face them, and somehow I would have to?

And all of this was happening less than twenty-four hours before the walk.

RESURRECTING A DREAM

I hung up with the producer and headed back to the room. Everything was wrapping up; Dan was packing his guitar while others were gathering their things. I said good night to everyone, but Erendira knew something was wrong. As I said my final good night, she took a seat on the couch in the room.

(Quick note to readers: As I recall these moments and sit to write them, I can feel my heart quicken again!)

"Nik, what's wrong?" she asked.

I looked at her for a moment, my stomach churning.

"The producers called. Unfortunately, the helicopter can't fly because the winds are so bad. You can't perform."

She looked at me, fighting back tears, and said, "I've just got to remain humble."

I didn't know what to say, and neither did she. I knew this opportunity to show the world some of *her* gifts was important to her, to both of us. She stood up and went to take a shower while I knelt down to pray.

"Lord, just give me wisdom on how we can fix this."

As I prayed, I began thinking what we could do to salvage her hard work. If the helicopter wasn't going to happen, what other options might we have? Then I remembered something that the riggers had thought of as a possibility for getting out to the middle of the wire to secure the stabilizers. Essentially, they came up with a plan where they increased the tension on my tether line above the wire and used it to move out across the main wire. If we could get the rigging team back out and have them increase the tension on the tether line, then Erendira might be able to go out on that and still perform on her lyra. I knew from an engineering perspective that it would work—Erendira wasn't nearly as heavy as a cart with two riggers inside it—and it would be a pretty cool shot for the camera. Not as great as a helicopter, but still pretty fantastic.

There were only two questions in my mind: Would Erendira go for it? And would my network partner?

I knew I could get the answer to the first question, so I went to the bathroom and called through the door, "I have an idea. What if I hang you on the tether cable and you perform from there?"

Erendira cracked the door. "I don't know. Is it going to look stupid? Is it safe? Do you even think you can make it work?"

"Yeah," I replied. "I think we can do it. Are you willing to give it a shot?"

She paused for a moment. "Yes!"

I went back into the bedroom and called Mark Bracco, the executive producer. I said, "Okay—I have a backup plan for Erendira." He was all ears, so I ran it past him, explaining how she could use the tether cable and what we'd need to do to make it safe. There was a pause.

Finally he said, "I don't know. I'll need to run it by everybody, but I don't know how comfortable I am with last-minute rigging and adjusting. I don't know how you could possibly pull that off."

I thanked Mark for being honest with me and hung up so he could make his calls. I knew there was a strong chance the network wouldn't like the idea because, as a general practice, they don't like last-minute anything. They like knowing everything in advance. At the same time, I was extremely confident we could pull it off because we had Maikol Munoz on our side. He was not only manager of the engineering company SIME S.A. but was also an engineer. Maikol had already gone above and beyond to make the wire safe. We wouldn't have been able to rig it and make it happen without him. So while the producer was making his calls, I called Maikol and said, "I've got an idea for replacing the helicopter stunt."

He said, "Good, because I saw the test flight, and there's no way your wife can fly in it."

"Agreed. So here's what I'm thinking: if we hang her on the tether line, we can tension it so it's well above the wire. Then we can pull her out toward the middle and she can perform, and then we pull her back in."

Without hesitating, Maikol said, "We can do that. I can figure something out. I'll make it happen for you."

From that moment on, I was in planning mode. I was mulling over rigging ideas and backup plans in my head all night, trying to think of every little detail and how we could make it work safely. As a result, I probably slept for an hour, maybe an hour and a half. Typically, I like to get a full night's rest before a walk, but this required more from me. As the hours ticked away, I finally said, "Okay, we're all going out there at 8:00 a.m. Everybody, all my crew, let's go out there together and get this done."

When the alarm went off, I got up and got dressed and went downstairs with my family for breakfast; then I took off for the volcano. When we arrived, Maikol's team had not arrived yet, but I immediately got out of the car and got started. As I was hooking the lyra onto the wire, a really cool moment unfolded before my eyes. My dad was up on top of the wire, hard at work. It was the first time I'd seen my dad set foot on a wire in at least fifteen or twenty years, but there he was, charging forward to help me and the family. It was a short time, but while we were both on the wire, we were able to get some cool photos that I will always cherish.

After a lot of work, we tied the lyra to the wire and Erendira climbed onto it. We sent her off to the middle of the wire, and it worked without a problem!

We kept checking and rechecking things through-out the afternoon, and suddenly it was almost showtime. The broadcast would start at 8:00 p.m. Eastern Time, but because Nicaragua is in the Central time zone, we would start at 7:00 p.m. on-site.

That was the first time in my career that I'd ever spent most of the day on the site of one of my walks. I always stay away until I have to be on-site for makeup, and even then, I prefer to get makeup and go straight to the wire.

Not on this day. There was a volcano and an inter-national broadcast awaiting us all.

———— • ◆ • ————

By 2:00 p.m., I needed to head back to the hotel for a few minutes of rest before getting dressed and ready. I usually get a chance to catch a quick nap the afternoon of the walk, but even as exhausted as I was, my mind was racing so fast that there was no rest to be had.

By 5:30 p.m., we loaded up for the drive back to the volcano.

I was staring out the window with Erendira, who was there at my side in the back of the car. So many big things for our entire family hung in the balance over the next few hours. I leaned forward, overwhelmed, my head pressed against the glass. Suddenly my phone rang. I looked down, saw a 202 number I didn't recognize, and bypassed the call. A few seconds later, that same number popped up, and I remembered that 202 is the area code for Washington, DC. I answered it. The voice on the other end was a woman.

"Is this Nik Wallenda?"

I said, "Yes, ma'am."

"Could you please hold for the president?"

The phone went silent as she put me on hold. So I quickly asked my daughter to pull out her phone and record. A few seconds later, the phone crackled to life and I heard the voice of President Donald Trump wishing me good luck.

Our conversation lasted less than a minute, but I can't tell you how encouraging that phone call was to me. It lifted my spirits up and away from the anxieties.

I looked at my wife and laughed a little. "Can you believe it?" I asked. "I'm just Nik Wallenda, that little boy who grew up performing as a clown and doing a dog act in county fairs and circuses—and today I got a call from the president of the United States. Wow . . ."

———— ◆ ————

Less than ninety minutes later, the cameras were rolling and the hosts, Chris Harrison and Sage Steele, were beginning to tell the live audience our family story. A few minutes later, they were sending my wife out over the crater of the volcano.

As the cameras and production teams worked furiously, I stayed focused on Erendira and how proud I was that the evening was going to start with her. All I can remember was looking out at Erendira, my heart beating with pride. She was amazing and gorgeous. I enjoyed every minute of watching her show off her skill and artistry to the world. For everything we had to do to salvage that performance, she made every single minute worth it. She inspires me.

But then she came off the wire, and it was my turn.

At this point, I was a bundle of energy. I was ready to get up on the wire and get started. Over the past three days, I'd dealt with a lot of stress—overwhelming stress—and it's not an understatement to say it felt at times like ten thousand pounds were pressing down on my chest. Everything that had happened over the weeks leading up to it all had torn down my psyche. I worked so hard to mentally build myself up by visualizing the walk—in my mind, I'd walked that cable a thousand times—but now it was happening for real. I did a quick interview after Erendira came down, said a family prayer, and then climbed into a truck for the drive around to my starting platform. I had my playlist cued up in the sound truck, so I asked the crew to start a motivational speech by Pastor Steven Furtick called "I Will Fight." They piped it into my earpiece, and I listened to that on the entire drive. "The Christian life is not a playground," Furtick's voice screamed into my ear. "It is a battleground. So today, I will give no place to fear or failure . . ."[1]

When I got to the other side, I stepped out of the truck fully energized and ready to walk. The producers had agreed that I would get out of the truck, put on my wire shoes, put on my gas mask and goggles, and then climb up a pyramid structure to the platform. Once at the top, I would ask my dad and Uncle Mike to check the wind and the tension, and if everything was good, I would be cleared to go. That's exactly the way I wanted it. I want to hit the platform and go; I don't want to step back, I don't want to pause, I don't want to stand and ponder. I just want to go.

I climbed to the top of the pyramid, wire shoes on, gas mask on, goggles on, and as I got to the top, the producer's voice came into my ear, saying, "We need a full three and a half minutes for commercial."

I replied, "Are you *serious*?"

"Yeah, we're going to commercial."

I couldn't help myself. "Listen, we talked about this, and you told me that I could just go on once I got up here. Now I'm here, my psyche and nerves are a mess, and you guys are sitting in an air-conditioned control room thinking everything is great. You're not thinking about what this does to me mentally or what this does to my goggles and my gas mask or oxygen. While you're running four minutes of commercials, that's four minutes of my safety that you've compromised. This is so unfair."

Nothing but silence on the other end.

I made the decision right there that the moment we came back from commercial, I was stepping out on the wire. The commercials wrapped up, the producer told me to get ready, and before she could say anything else, I walked out. I told the audio engineers to turn my worship music up in my ear, and from that point on, I was focused on the wire. I locked into my music and put one foot in front of the other, allowing myself to get used to the walk. After the first thirty feet I noticed two things: First, I needed to look at the lava below because it was absolutely breathtaking. So much so, I mentioned it as I was walking. The second thing was that the wire felt pretty darn good. But as I was looking down at the lava and noticing the wire, I also noticed the labels on my stabilizer cables. I knew that they were spaced out every thirty feet, which meant I could now calculate how far I'd traveled.

When I walk, I prefer not to know how far along I am—I just want to know that the next step will bring me that much closer to the other side. It's a way of keeping my concentration, of keeping my mind and body locked into the here and now, which keeps me safe. If you were to watch my Grand Canyon special, there's a point where my dad calls out and tells me that I'm about halfway, and I reply something like "Dad, I don't want to know, because I don't want to break my concentration!" For as often as I've done this, there's definitely great fear and anxiety each time I go up, which is why I always quote the scripture, "Be anxious for nothing" (Phil. 4:6 NKJV).

In preparation for the volcano walk, I had practiced the distance—1,800 feet—hundreds of times in my backyard. I knew that distance should take me about twenty-three minutes to cover. But as we were working with the production team from ABC, they let me know that when it came time for me to walk, they wanted me to take thirty minutes. Statistics from previous walks had shown that the longer I was out on the wire, the higher the ratings climbed.

So I knew that I needed to walk a little slower than my

typical pace. I wanted to do so, though, with complete concentration on the wire and the walk, not on the clock or the distance, which meant that staring at the stabilizer markers wasn't helping.

I quickly forced myself to focus back on my worship music and on every step. Concentrating on those two things was helping me, but being out on the wire in a hyperaware state was tough. I noticed a number eight, which meant I was 240 feet out. I looked ahead and saw the nine marker, so 270 feet was closing fast, and that would put me near the point where the stabilizer wires were anchored differently, which in turn meant the tension and stability of the wire were about to change as well.

The subtle change in the wires translated into my feet, and I began to freak out because of the way the wire was moving. Panic shot up, but I thought about how my training wire in Sarasota was much worse.

It was about there that several things hit at once: I was getting closer to the thick of the gases right as the wire started moving more rapidly and a crazy gust of wind hit me hard. I stopped for a second before telling myself, *Okay, when the next gust of wind hits, just keep walking, keep walking.* I was nowhere close to the center of the crater yet, but this storm had come in, and it was strong. It wasn't worse than I expected, but it was certainly different from what I expected, and it was definitely worse than I wanted.

I walked a little farther as the conditions worsened and thought, *You know what? I'm not going to stop to brace for the winds anymore. I'm just going to press on.* At that point, I'd stopped twice to catch my balance and adjust to the gases and the wind, which would blow in like a tornado for one second and then vanish, making the air really, really hot and then really, really cool—like an eerie cool. So I decided that I simply wouldn't stop the rest of the way. I would just keep moving.

On the very next step, as I raised my foot, a gust of wind pushed me back so violently that I thought I was going to be pushed onto my back. In fact, it was so strong that I struggled to land my foot back on the wire. In that moment, I felt like the apostle Peter walking on water—he stepped out of a boat onto a stormy lake, and when the wind whipped around him, he took his eyes off Jesus and began to sink. At that point, Peter cried out to Jesus, who reached out and grabbed him. I didn't want to get distracted by the wind. I didn't want to take my eyes off of God.

Candidly, I need a little wind and waves when I walk. I need the tension to help keep the audience engaged, so even when I was praying about the conditions above the volcano prior to the walk, I never prayed for no gases or wind. Instead I prayed for manageable wind and manageable gases; I didn't want to walk over a volcano and have someone say, "Oh, he just walked over a volcano, but it wasn't a very active volcano." But in that moment, as my foot frantically searched for the wire, I thought, *God, maybe this is a little more excitement than I bargained for.*

At this same moment, I heard something in my ear that shook me to my core: my wife, who was watching on a screen because I was so far away from the finish and the gases were so thick that she couldn't see me with her own eyes, said, "I gotta walk away, guys. I'm sorry. I can't watch anymore." She was standing next to my dad, and his mic was open, which is why I heard the feed in my ear. It scared me; if Erendira couldn't watch—if she was unnerved from her vantage point—then it must have looked even worse than what I was experiencing. What was she seeing that made her so worried about my safety? What lay ahead?

What was I walking into?

The answer turned out to be the middle of the volcano's cauldron, where the steam and gas became overwhelming. As those elements hit me, fear threatened to overwhelm me, right there on the wire, suspended above a pool of molten lava. For all the progress I'd made, for all of the things I'd learned, that moment seemed capable of undoing me, perhaps for good. But I thought of Peter once more, realized I needed to focus on God, and prayed, "God, I know you control the wind and the waves, and I know you are here with me and you are in control."

Almost instantly, a peace filled my heart. The overwhelming fear was replaced by an overwhelming joy, and I started thanking and worshiping God and kept going. I knew that's what Erendira would tell me to do, so I continued on, using the stabilizer markers to get me from one point to the next. There were four transitions for the stabilizer wires, causing me to have to adjust my balance uniquely at each one. As I got to the middle, the wire was at its sloppiest, moving all around, forcing me to really lean into my training and my faith in order to keep one foot in front of the other.

After I was two-thirds of the way across, I actually did begin thinking about time, about what I would do if I was ahead of pace, about what I could possibly do on the wire to add excitement if I needed to be slower. I thought, if the wire got better, then I'd possibly be able to sit down, do some push-ups, or do something special. I was thinking about all of this while talking to the hosts, when suddenly my dad said, "You can speed it up a bit."

I felt relieved that I didn't need to slow down for production purposes but also had absolutely no intention of speeding up, either. After all I'd been through, I was going to take every step carefully until I reached the other side. As I got closer to the other side of the cauldron, I began thanking God for bringing me through the fire and through the storm and for allowing me to make it safely across. All of my praise—including my singing of several songs on my soundtrack—was captured on live television because the network kept my microphone open during the entire walk.

Nearing the end, while still on the wire, I ripped off my goggles, then my gas mask, and as I finally crossed over solid ground, I let my balance pole fall as well. I was tired. Even as Chris and Sage interviewed me, and my family gathered around for hugs, there was a mixture of celebration and exhaustion within my body.

I had completed the longest and most dangerous walk of my career, but more than that, I had faced my fears on the wire in a way I'd never done before. I navigated one of the most stressful and frightening seasons of my life thanks to what I'd learned in the years since that fall in Sarasota. It was certainly like nothing else I've ever done, and given the intensity of the battle, it may be unlike anything I ever do again.

But I had done it.

CHAPTER 14

A RELIABLE PROCESS YOU CAN EASILY REPEAT

WHEN I TOOK THE WIRE IN MASAYA, I BECAME AWARE of something I'd not expected. More than the heat, more than the gases, more than the length of the walk or the cameras or the wind, I was aware of how totally at peace I was. Even after such a long and crazy and frustrating day, when I took that first step out over the cauldron, I wasn't at war with anything. I was completely at peace. And that was only true because I finally knew how to face my fear and overcome it.

As I neared the walk's end, I could see my wife and amazing children there waiting for me. I could see my father too. But one person whose presence had special meaning for me was Lijana. In 2017 she nearly died with me on the wire, then she fought fears and came back in Times Square and encouraged me to keep moving, stretching my limits.

After years of working so hard to identify, name, talk

to, and move past my fears, I realized at Masaya that I had developed and embraced a reliable process I could easily repeat whenever fear stuck out its ugly face. Walking across that wire gave me a greater sense of God's purpose and plan for my life, because I knew I had the tools necessary to prevent me from running scared and to embrace a deeper belief that my purpose is bigger than my fears or doubts.

I wish I could better describe it to you, but it was as if I could feel God answering *all* of those prayers I'd prayed and sung over myself—even when I didn't know that's what I was doing. There were so many things happening as I crossed that wire, bringing me full circle, redeeming yet another piece of my family's legacy by reminding me that God is always faithful, and that he is always in control. If this book is about nothing else, it's about remembering that truth above all others.

I opened this book with a story of a fall that no one expected, of a group of seasoned, trained professional aerialists tumbling through the air, helpless against the moment and gravity. It wasn't just some random story; it was *my* story, and I've done my best to share with you each step of my journey and help you get inside my quest. If you've read this far, though, you've discovered that this is more than my story.

This is your story too.

MAKE THE STORY YOUR OWN

You live out some part of this story every day, because facing and overcoming fear is a natural part of what it means to be human. The physical dimensions and demands of my story may not be at play in your life, but you've likely recognized yourself once or twice in this book. Together we've discovered some of the most common truths about facing and overcoming fear, but having that knowledge isn't enough—we must act on what we know if we want to defeat fear.

If you're going to make this story *your* story, then I want to remind you of the five big ideas that will help you truly take this material to heart.

1. We All Fall

I opened with the fall in Sarasota because all fear begins with an inciting incident. It may be a traumatic loss of life, a financial upheaval, or an unexpected medical diagnosis, but there is always something that triggers our fears and gives them power.

2. We All Fall Again

If our issues with fear stopped after the initial incident, things would be a lot easier. But fear doesn't come once and leave us for good; it comes in waves. Sometimes it's what we realize about the world after a loss—that we don't have control, no matter how much we try—that sends us deeper into the fear trap. For a long time I believed that if I prepared enough, I would always be in control of my fate on the wire, and maybe you've had similar ideas. Work hard enough, be good enough, serve often enough, be generous enough, and the world would yield to you. But only God is in control, and while we rest in that and can enjoy a personal relationship with him through his Son, Jesus, being close to God does not put us in control. It merely puts us next to the one who is. So we fall, and we fall again, not because God isn't in control but because we still believe we are (or want to be).

3. The Answer Is Growth

I hesitate to use the word *answer* here because we've been trained by our culture that an answer is essentially a one-time thing, a vaccination or special pill you take once to make all of your problems go away. Most answers don't work that way—if they did, engineers and builders would never say, "Measure twice, cut once." Sometimes, the answer for now isn't the answer for next week. But I'm choosing this word because of the other one it's paired with: *growth*.

When you are making an effort to grow every day—to get even 1 percent better than you were yesterday—then growth really is the answer to fear. Fear seeks to make you feel small. It seeks to keep you stuck in patterns, habits, and systems that don't serve you well or allow you to live with full freedom and joy. As long as fear feels bigger than you, there's a high probability it can win. But when you make an effort to grow daily—to read your Bible, change a habit, push yourself harder at work, be more attentive as a spouse or parent—you begin to get bigger on the inside. You begin to develop new confidence, new skills, new ways of seeing yourself and the world. Suddenly those same old fears aren't as big as they used to be because you're so much bigger by comparison.

Growth will push you to try new things, to fail at some things, and to keep looking for everything you need to become a better person. My growth journey was very individualized; yours might include more people. My journey happened very quickly; yours might take several years. But no matter how different our growth journeys may be, waking up every day and taking the next step in front of us is something we all must do in order to overcome fear.

4. You Must Develop Good Habits

I've been up front with you about my habits throughout this book, the little things I do that help me stay focused and disciplined. I've told you about my worship playlists that I develop as I'm practicing for a walk and how those songs effectively become prayers over me and the performance, giving me words to connect with God that I wouldn't otherwise be able to find. I've shared some insights into my training regimen, how I start the wire low and loose, or practice in simulated violent weather conditions. These aren't personality quirks; they're the lived-out expressions of what I believe. They are the physical examples of my mental foundation, or if you'd like a simpler term, they are my habits for self-discipline.

If you're going to grow and use that growth to overcome fear, you have to develop habits that can sustain you on the journey. Maybe you need an exercise routine, a better diet, a personal time for reflection, or regular visits with an experienced counselor. If you're not sure how to go about developing better habits, then start with the habits you have now and evaluate which ones work for you and which ones work against you. If the habit is helpful, ask yourself if there's some way it can be improved to serve you even more. If the habit is unhelpful, then ask if you're willing to give it up.

Evaluating habits can be challenging because we often design routines that are meant to keep us comfortable—and it takes a strong mind to willingly interrupt that comfort in order to build toward growth.

5. Step Out in Faith . . . Again

I'm most excited to revisit this idea, because it's the one, above all others, that keeps me focused. I wrote in chapter 11 about the need to focus on the future, sharing with you briefly how my dream has always been to come back to the circus and help it grow into the future.

Once upon a time, our culture saw the circus as magical; it was a place of fantastic sights and sounds and experiences that you couldn't find anywhere else. If you've ever taken a child to a circus, you know that magic still exists for the child—the colors, the spectacles, the endless joy of being part of a world unlike anything in real life. But the challenge for the circus business over the last fifty years has been how to keep the interest of those between the ages of twelve and twenty-four. How do you keep the circus cool for *that* demographic? Buried in that challenge is the opportunity to build something that lasts—and I have been fixated on it my whole life. Call me a little overconfident, but I've got ideas here that I believe in my soul will absolutely work.

Believe it or not, this is one of the things that went through my mind as I walked over Masaya. Where do you go after walking a live volcano? What trick could be bigger, more amazing, more awe-inspiring? Could it be starting my own circus?

For some, *circus* is a negative term that signifies chaos

and disorder and phoniness. We call people clowns when we want to minimize them, or we call crumbling businesses or failing governments a three-ring circus as a way of highlighting their dysfunction. What some people think of when they say *circus* has been reduced to anything other than magical. What would it take to reset their understanding of a circus? How amazing would it be to reintroduce them to the magic and wonder of the world where I grew up?

The truth is, a circus is one of the most organized, efficient, amazing places on earth. People don't appreciate how hard it is to make something so organized *look* disorganized! Having grown up in that world, I would happily challenge anyone to find an industry that can move nine hundred people from one location to another and build a literal city overnight. That's what the circus can do—and did do—for decades: it moved a massive collection of performers, workers, animals, tents, and equipment across miles of darkened road or railroad track, only to set up an astounding community twenty-four hours later. It was accomplished through genuine community, through people living and working together to take care of everyone's best interests. The circus thrived when that sense of community—that sense of family—was at its core because people will work tirelessly for those they love.

When I started my career, I was committed to a life in the circus. It was what I grew up knowing; it's what my family did for generations before me, and truthfully, under the big top is one of my favorite places to be. I looked at it the way a seventh-generation farmer or a fourth-generation basketball coach might look at life spent pursuing those careers. But over time, I realized that in order to enjoy life working under a tent later in my career, I needed to step away from that life for a bit and challenge myself to dream so big that I might one day help reinvent our business. If I was going to live a life that gave me the greatest opportunity to share the blessings God has given me, I was going to have to choose a different path. And so I did. My dream has grown and changed over the years, and there have been setbacks and breakdowns along the way, but in everything, I know I've done my best to move closer to the person I want to become and set my path to do exactly what I mentioned earlier: to one day help reshape opinions about my industry.

So launching my own circus is my next step of faith because there's fear in this dream—real and present fear. There's the economic fear that I could lose everything I have worked to build. I've worked so hard to build this nest egg, and it could all go away if I sink it into a circus. That fear speaks loudly, and it speaks with a hint of truth—I *could* lose everything. But that could happen no matter what I invest in; I could invest in a laundromat or a restaurant (and I've considered both of those ideas!) or buy shares in some of the most successful companies in the marketplace, and there's a chance I could still lose big. But that's the nature of investment—it requires risk to produce a return. I could choose not to invest at all, but just keeping my money in my account doesn't help me; it just builds up and it goes away, builds up and goes away. Without a dream to work for, it simply sits.

Yes, there's risk associated with launching my own circus, and yes, there's fear, but there's also the joy of fulfilling my lifelong dream. There's the feeling of having my own show filled with the people and life that I love, being watched and appreciated by thousands of people who have come to understand and reclaim the magic of the circus. My fears would cause me to miss out on all of that, and I can't let that happen. I have to keep pushing toward my dream—I have to keep pushing toward my own circus.

After Times Square, when I was thinking about my next step, my next big move, I was kicking ideas around with my family. I knew what my next big walk would be—walking over Masaya—but Erendira pulled me aside and brought up starting a circus again.

"I think now is the time," she said.

"Why?" I asked.

"The kids are close to graduating, and your name is established. We can pull this together and finally bring our dream to life. And besides," she said, "we're not getting any younger. This is it."

She was right. While we prepared for Masaya and what was my most dangerous televised walk ever, I also started planning to face my most dangerous business decision too. I began contacting manufacturers and financers and started working on what exactly it would take for me to get my show out of my head and into the real world. I began taking these small next steps of faith because they are what keep me growing, keep me learning, keep me ahead of my fears.

Three days after I came home from Masaya, I hopped on a plane to San Diego and met with a circus tent manufacturer. After spending the day together talking about design and production and other technical aspects, we shook hands and I walked away the owner of a brand-new, honest-to-goodness circus big top that will soon find its home in Sarasota, Florida. It's going to take some time and some careful planning, but eventually Nik Wallenda's Zirkus will open to the public with a reimagined view of what the circus can and should be in the modern world. And if you're wondering about the spelling, that's a little nod to my great-grandfather, Karl, a bright German man who saw possibility and purpose in the circus industry—a vision and a gift he has passed along to me.

———— • ◆ • ————

My friends, you can face your fears and overcome them. You are not broken beyond repair, nor is there a night so dark that the light of hope cannot find you. If you'll hold to the reliable process in this chapter and the teachings within this book, you no longer have to be a slave to fear. If, however, your fears still feel far too big for you handle, then may I encourage you with one more thing?

No matter your fears, no matter how big they seem or how powerful they feel, there is a Father God who loves you more than you know, and he sent his only Son, Jesus Christ, to die in your place, to pay the penalty for your sins. For all who believe in the name of Jesus, the Bible says that he will live within us, and when Jesus lives in us, we no longer have "the spirit of fear; but of power, and of love, and of a sound mind" (2 Tim. 1:7 KJV).

This is God's free gift to you. I encourage you to take it.

It is nothing short of amazing.

ACKNOWLEDGMENTS

FIRST AND FOREMOST, I WANT TO ACKNOWLEDGE MY Lord and Savior, Jesus Christ. I am so grateful for your love, which is steadfast even when I fail. Through the darkest time in my life, Jesus, you reminded me that you are always there. When I was a young person, you impressed on my heart that you would bless me beyond my wildest dreams, and you have done so in more ways than I could ever imagine.

Erendira, how amazing it is that God blessed me with someone who not only could understand my dreams but would join me in them. You've been my biggest encourager and supporter, my confidante, my adviser, and my best friend. Your love for God and his Word inspires me, and you helped guide me back to his peace during dark times.

My sons, Yanni and Amadaos, thank you for teaching me the highest level of courage as you stepped out to serve our country in the armed forces. I beam with pride even as I write this. You are braver than I will ever be!

My daughter, Evita, thank you for the joy and laughter

you bring to each day. As you start your senior year of high school and begin to make plans to pursue your dreams, know that I am always here to support you . . . even if that includes making TikTok videos!

Mom and Dad, you literally taught me the ropes. You taught me to be driven in my skill, to prove to you that I took my art seriously, and that I was ready to perform with you. I'm grateful that you are at every one of my walks, praying for me, ensuring my rigging is safe, and literally talking me through each step.

Lijana, thank you for always being there for me growing up. You are such an inspiration to me. We helped each other through perhaps the most difficult time in our lives, and hugging you at the end of our walk in New York was one of the greatest moments of my life.

Don Yaeger, you take the words out of my mouth! You've been brilliant, placing in print the thoughts that were sometimes so hard for me to express. I am proud to now call you a friend. I pray that our work together will inspire many who read this book! Thanks, too, to your teammate Jason Brooks.

My managers, Winston and David, thanks for stepping out of the comfort zone of your industry to take a chance on the wild dreams of a young wire walker. You helped take my career to another level and played a monumental role in relieving that "fear of feathers."

Lonnie, thanks for always encouraging me to take my dreams one step further than I can envision on my own. You should always know that I have your back (well, that is if it means waxing your back anyways). I'm here for ya!

Joseph, thank you for always being there and supporting me in everything I do! I wouldn't be where I am today without your endless support. Whenever I'm in a bind, I know I can count on you to have my back.

Uncle Mike, thank you for bringing your engineering talents out of retirement to help my visions become reality. We've spanned some of the most incredible skylines and natural wonders together.

Pastor Randy and Pastor Burnard, thank you for your godly wisdom, spiritual guidance, and friendship in some of the most trying times of my life. From praying together in the hospital to hours of counsel and conversation, I can always count on you both. Thank you to the entire Bayside Community Church family as well for praying over each step I took across the wire over Times Square and the Masaya volcano.

To the other members of the eight-person pyramid, Nicholas Slimick, Blake Wallenda, Alec Bryant, Andrew Adams, Zebulon Fricke, and Aunt Rietta—when I was ready to give up, you told me to get back on the wire, and so many of you joined me again in performances to follow. Thank you.

To the first responders who came to the tent following our accident; SMH trauma surgeons Dr. Alan Brockhurst and Dr. Ali Al-Rawi; and all the medical staff of the Sarasota Memorial Hospital, Lakewood Ranch Medical Center, and Blake Medical Center who attended to my family following the accident—we are forever grateful for the care you took to help us on the path to recovery so that we could continue doing what we love.

ACKNOWLEDGMENTS

Maikol Munoz, my dream of walking over the Masaya volcano would not have been possible without the incredible work of you and your crew. You worked tirelessly, making sure everything was precise and correct. When there were challenges, you never despaired; you helped us find solutions even on the day of the event.

Edgard Torres, my walk over Masaya would not have been possible without you. Thank you for the thread that wove all the parties together that would be required to make it happen.

Scott Igoe, thanks for believing in my wild dreams to walk over Times Square and the Masaya volcano, and for playing a key role in bringing them to the world on live TV!

The entire team at Dick Clark Productions, thank you for bringing your professionalism and expertise in live television event production to my walks. You were incredible partners, and I can't wait to do it again.

Finally, to the team at HarperCollins Christian Publishing, including publisher Damon Reiss, acquisitions editor Kyle Olund, and senior editor Meaghan Porter—thanks for making this book real.

NOTES

Chapter 1: The Fall

1. "Wallendas Have Tragic History in Detroit," *Detroit Free Press*, November 3, 2014, https://www.freep.com/story/news/local /michigan/detroit/2014/11/03/wallendas-fatal-fall-detroit -circus/18405583/.

2. "Why Being Able to Compartmentalize Is a Key Ingredient for Risk-Taking," Knowledge@Wharton, January 14, 2014, https://knowledge.wharton.upenn.edu/article/able -compartmentalize-key-ingredient-risk-taking/.

Chapter 2: The Second Fall

1. "Understanding the Stress Response," Harvard Health Publishing— Harvard Medical School, updated May 1, 2018, https://www.health .harvard.edu/staying-healthy/understanding-the-stress-response.

2. Kendra Cherry, "How the Fight or Flight Response Works," VeryWellMind, updated August 18, 2019, https://www .verywellmind.com/what-is-the-fight-or-flight-response-2795194.

3. Steph Solis, "Ringling Bros. Circus Closing After 146 Years," *USA Today*, January 14, 2017, https://www.usatoday.com /story/news/nation/2017/01/14/ringling-bros-circus-close -after-146-years/96606820/.

Chapter 3: Knowing Is Not Enough

1. Jennifer Huizen, "Feeling Numb: What You Need to Know," Medical News Today, November 17, 2017, https://www.medicalnewstoday.com/articles/320049.php#what-are-the-causes.

Chapter 5: Worship on the Wire

1. Josh Baldwin, vocalist, "Stand in Your Love," by Ethan Hulse, Josh Baldwin, Mark Harris, and Rita Springer, on *Without Words: Genesis*, Bethel Music, 2019.
2. Substance Abuse and Mental Health Services Administration (SAMHSA), "Understanding the Impact of Trauma," chap. 3 in *Trauma-Informed Care in Behavioral Health Services, Treatment Improvement Protocol (TIP)*, no. 57 (Rockville, MD: Center for Substance Abuse Treatment, 2014), 61, https://www.ncbi.nlm.nih.gov/books/NBK207191/.
3. Richard J. Foster, "Understanding Worship," in Nathan Foster, *The Making of an Ordinary Saint: My Journey from Frustration to Joy with the Spiritual Disciplines* (Grand Rapids: Monarch Books, 2014), 167.
4. "No Longer Slaves," by Jonathan Helser, Joel Case, and Brian Johnson, on *We Will Not Be Shaken*, Bethel Music, 2014.
5. Sofia Seinfeld et al., "Influence of Music on Anxiety Induced by Fear of Heights in Virtual Reality," *Frontiers in Psychology* 6, no. 1969 (January 2016), https://www.frontiersin.org/articles/10.3389/fpsyg.2015.01969/full.
6. Seinfeld et al., "Influence of Music."
7. Seinfeld et al., "Influence of Music."

Chapter 7: Walking Toward Healing

1. Kelly McCarthy, "Nik Wallenda Calls Sister's High-Wire Stunt After Major Accident 'Almost Impossible,'" GMA, June 20, 2019, https://www.goodmorningamerica.com/culture/story/nik-lijana-wallenda-talk-attempted-times-square-high-63804055.

Chapter 8: Fear of Feathers

1. You can learn more about the Ronald McDonald House mission at https://www.rmhc.org/what-we-do.
2. "Wallenda, at Wisconsin State Fair, Completes His Longest Tightrope Walk," *Chicago Tribune*, August 12, 2015, https://www.chicagotribune.com/news/ct-wallenda-tightrope-wisconsin-state-fair-20150811-story.html.

Chapter 9: Face Your Fear

1. "Facts and Statistics," Anxiety and Depression Association of America, accessed March 10, 2020, https://adaa.org/about-adaa/press-room/facts-statistics.
2. "Facts and Statistics."

Chapter 10: Find Your Footing

1. Nicole Spector, "Smiling Can Trick Your Brain into Happiness—and Boost Your Health," NBC News Better, November 28, 2017, https://www.nbcnews.com/better/health/smiling-can-trick-your-brain-happiness-boost-your-health-ncna822591.

Chapter 11: Focus on Your Future

1. "About Cirque," Cirque du Soleil, https://www.cirquedusoleil.com/press/kits/corporate/about-cirque.
2. "History," Cirque du Soleil, https://www.cirquedusoleil.com/about-us/history.
3. "Coronavirus Pushes Cirque du Soleil to Explore Options Including Bankruptcy—Sources," Fox Business, March 26, 2020, https://www.foxbusiness.com/economy/coronavirus-pushes-cirque-du-soleil-to-explore-options-including-bankruptcy-sources.
4. "Coronavirus Pushes Cirque du Soleil."

Chapter 13: Fresh Steps of Faith

1. Steven Furtick, "I Will Fight," released March 26, 2014, YouTube, 3:14, https://www.youtube.com/watch?v=uC0FNOm26NU.

ABOUT THE AUTHORS

NIK WALLENDA IS A SEVENTH-GENERATION MEMBER of the legendary Wallenda family. Known worldwide for his incredible feats on the high wire and beyond, Nik has held seven Guinness World Records, among them the highest four-level eight-person pyramid on the wire, the highest and longest bicycle ride on a wire, and the highest altitude while hanging from a helicopter by his teeth.

Nik's career began at the age of two, as he learned to walk the wire while holding his mother's hand, and led from there to record-breaking performances across the United States and around the world. In 2012, Nik fulfilled his lifelong dream to become the only person to walk directly over the precipice of Niagara Falls, which was broadcast live by ABC. In 2013, he became the first person to walk a wire across the Grand Canyon, an epic event aired live by the Discovery Channel in 178 countries, breaking network ratings and social media records in the process. The next Discovery special took place in Chicago, where he walked blindfolded between two skyscrapers in November 2014. In

June 2019, accompanied by his sister, Lijana Wallenda, Nik became the first person to walk over New York City's Times Square, an event carried live on ABC. In March 2020, he took to the airwaves again, walking over an active volcano live on ABC.

Nik's motto is "Never give up," and he carries this positive message with him in every walk with the purpose of inspiring people around the world to follow their dreams.

DON YAEGER IS AN ELEVEN-TIME *NEW YORK TIMES* bestselling author, a longtime associate editor at *Sports Illustrated*, and an inspirational speaker. He lives in Tallahassee, Florida, with his wife, son, and daughter.